CBSE Term II 2022

Computer Applications

Class X

Complete Theory in Sync with Syllabus

Case Based Questions

Short/Long Answer Questions

3 Practice Papers with Explanations

Author
Neetu Gaikwad

✿ arihant

ARIHANT PRAKASHAN (School Division Series)

ARIHANT PRAKASHAN (School Division Series)

ॐ **Administrative & Production Offices**

Regd. Office
'Ramchhaya' 4577/15, Agarwal Road, Darya Ganj, New Delhi -110002
Tele: 011- 47630600, 43518550

ॐ **Head Office**
Kalindi, TP Nagar, Meerut (UP) - 250002, Tel: 0121-7156203, 7156204

ॐ **Sales & Support Offices**
Agra, Ahmedabad, Bengaluru, Bareilly, Chennai, Delhi, Guwahati, Hyderabad, Jaipur, Jhansi, Kolkata, Lucknow, Nagpur & Pune.

ॐ **ISBN :** 978-93-25796-70-6

ॐ **PRICE :** ₹125.00

PO No : TXT-XX-XXXXXXX-X-XX

Published by Arihant Publications (India) Ltd.

For further information about the books published by Arihant, log on to www.arihantbooks.com or e-mail at info@arihantbooks.com

Follow us on    

Contents

Watch Free Learning Videos

Subscribe **arihant** YouTube Channel

- ☑ Video Solutions of CBSE Sample Papers
- ☑ Chapterwise Important MCQs
- ☑ CBSE Updates

Syllabus
CBSE Term II Class X

Computer Applications

Unit No.	Units	Marks
1.	Networking	15
2.	HTML	10

UNIT-1 Networking

- Internet: World Wide Web, web servers, web clients, websites, web pages, web browsers, blogs, news groups, HTML, web address, e-mail address, downloading and uploading files from a remote site. Internet protocols: TCP/IP, SMTP, POP3, HTTP, HTTPS. Remote login and file transfer protocols: SSH, SFTP, FTP, SCP, TELNET, SMTP, TCP/IP.

- Services available on the internet: information retrieval, locating sites using search engines and finding people on the net;

- Web services: chat, e-mail, video conferencing, e-Learning, e-Banking, e-Shopping, e-Reservation, e-Governance, e-Groups, social networking.

- Mobile technologies: SMS, MMS, 3G, 4G.

UNIT-2 HTML - II

- Embed audio and video in a HTML page.

- Create a table using the tags: table, tr, th, td, rowspan, colspan

- Links: significance of linking, anchor element (attributes: href, mailto), targets.

- Cascading style sheets: colour, background-colour, border-style, margin, height, width, outline, font (family, style, size), align, float

CBSE Circular

Exam Scheme Term I & II

केन्द्रीय माध्यमिक शिक्षा बोर्ड
(शिक्षा मंत्रालय, भारत सरकार के अधीन एक स्वायत संगठन)

CENTRAL BOARD OF SECONDARY EDUCATION
(An Autonomous Organisation under the Ministry of Education, Govt. of India)

CBSE/DIR (ACAD)/2021

Date: July 05, 2021
Circular No: Acad-51/2021

All the Heads of Schools affiliated to CBSE

Subject: Special Scheme of Assessment for Board Examination Classes X and XII for the Session 2021-22

COVID 19 pandemic caused almost all CBSE schools to function in a virtual mode for most part of the academic session of 2020-21. Due to the extreme risk associated with the conduct of Board examinations during the second wave in April 2021, CBSE had to cancel both its class X and XII Board examinations of the year 2021 and results are to be declared on the basis of a credible, reliable, flexible and valid alternative assessment policy. This, in turn, also necessitated deliberations over alternative ways to look at the learning objectives as well as the conduct of the Board Examinations for the academic session 2021-22 in case the situation remains unfeasible.

CBSE has also held stake holder consultations with Government schools as well as private independent schools from across the country especially schools from the remote rural areas and a majority of them have requested for the rationalization of the syllabus, similar to last year in view of reduced time permitted for organizing online classes. The Board has also considered the concerns regarding differential availability of electronic gadgets, connectivity and effectiveness of online teaching and other socio-economic issues specially with respect to students from economically weaker section and those residing in far flung areas of the country. In a survey conducted by CBSE, it was revealed that the rationalized syllabus notified for the session 2020-21 was effective for schools in covering the syllabus and helped learners in achieving learning objectives in a less stressful manner.

In the above backdrop and in line with the Board's continued focus on assessing stipulated learning outcomes by making the examinations competencies and core concepts based, student-centric, transparent, technology-driven, and having advance provision of alternatives for different future scenarios, the following schemes are introduced for the Academic Session for Class X and Class XII 2021-22.

केन्द्रीय माध्यमिक शिक्षा बोर्ड

(शिक्षा मंत्रालय, भारत सरकार के अधीन एक स्वायत संगठन)

CENTRAL BOARD OF SECONDARY EDUCATION

(An Autonomous Organisation under the Ministryof Education, Govt. of India)

Special Scheme for 2021-22

A. Academic session to be divided into 2 Terms with approximately 50% syllabus in each term:

The syllabus for the Academic session 2021-22 will be divided into 2 terms by following a systematic approach by looking into the interconnectivity of concepts and topics by the Subject Experts and the Board will conduct examinations at the end of each term on the basis of the bifurcated syllabus. This is done to increase the probability of having a Board conducted classes X and XII examinations at the end of the academic session.

B. The syllabus for the Board examination 2021-22 will be rationalized similar to that of the last academic session to be notified in July 2021. For academic transactions, however, schools will follow the curriculum and syllabus released by the Board vide Circular no. F.1001/CBSE-Acad/Curriculum/2021 dated 31 March 2021. Schools will also use alternative academic calendar and inputs from the NCERT on transacting the curriculum.

C. Efforts will be made to make Internal Assessment/ Practical/ Project work more credible and valid as per the guidelines and Moderation Policy to be announced by the Board to ensure fair distribution of marks.

Details of Curriculum Transaction

- Schools will continue teaching in distance mode till the authorities permit in-person mode of teaching in schools.
- **Classes IX-X: Internal Assessment** (throughout the year-irrespective of Term I and II) would include the *3 periodic tests, student enrichment, portfolio and practical work/ speaking listening activities/ project.*
- **Classes XI-XII: Internal Assessment** (throughout the year-irrespective of Term I and II) would include end of topic or unit tests/ exploratory activities/ practicals/ projects.
- Schools would create a student profile for all assessment undertaken over the year and retain the evidences in digital format.
- CBSE will facilitate schools to upload marks of Internal Assessment on the CBSE IT platform.
- Guidelines for Internal Assessment for all subjects will also be released along with the rationalized term wise divided syllabus for the session 2021-22.The Board would also provide additional resources like sample assessments, question banks, teacher training etc. for more reliable and valid internal assessments.

केन्द्रीय माध्यमिक शिक्षा बोर्ड

(शिक्षा मंत्रालय, भारत सरकार के अधीन एक स्वायत संगठन)

CENTRAL BOARD OF SECONDARY EDUCATION

(An Autonomous Organisation under the Ministryof Education, Govt. of India)

Term I Examinations:

- At the end of the first term, the Board will organize **Term I Examination** in a flexible schedule to be conducted between November-December 2021 with a window period of 4-8 weeks for schools situated in different parts of country and abroad. Dates for conduct of examinations will be notified subsequently.

- The Question Paper will have Multiple Choice Questions (MCQ) including case-based MCQs and MCQs on assertion-reasoning type. Duration of test will be **90 minutes** and it will cover only the rationalized syllabus of **Term I only** (i.e. approx. 50% of the entire syllabus).

- Question Papers will be sent by the CBSE to schools along with marking scheme.

- The exams will be conducted under the supervision of the External Center Superintendents and Observers appointed by CBSE.

- The responses of students will be captured on OMR sheets which, after scanning may be directly uploaded at CBSE portal or alternatively may be evaluated and marks obtained will be uploaded by the school on the very same day. The final direction in this regard will be conveyed to schools by the Examination Unit of the Board.

- Marks of the **Term I** Examination will contribute to the final overall score of students.

Term II Examination/ Year-end Examination:

- At the end of the second term, the Board would organize **Term II or Year-end Examination** based on the rationalized syllabus of Term II only (i.e. approximately 50% of the entire syllabus).

- This examination would be held around **March-April 2022** at the examination centres fixed by the Board.

- The paper will be of **2 hours duration** and have questions of different formats (case-based/ situation based, open ended- short answer/ long answer type).

- In case the situation is not conducive for normal descriptive examination a **90 minute MCQ based exam** will be conducted at the end of the Term II also.

- Marks of the Term II Examination would contribute to the final overall score.

केन्द्रीय माध्यमिक शिक्षा बोर्ड

(शिक्षा मंत्रालय, भारत सरकार के अधीन एक स्वायत संगठन)

CENTRAL BOARD OF SECONDARY EDUCATION

(An Autonomous Organisation under the Ministryof Education, Govt. of India)

Assessment / Examination as per different situations

A. In case the situation of the pandemic improves and students are able to come to schools or centres for taking the exams.

Board would conduct Term I and Term II examinations at schools/centres and the theory marks will be distributed equally between the two exams.

B. In case the situation of the pandemic forces complete closure of schools during November-December 2021, but Term II exams are held at schools or centres.

Term I MCQ based examination would be done by students online/offline from home - in this case, the weightage of this exam for the final score would be reduced, and weightage of Term II exams will be increased for declaration of final result.

C. In case the situation of the pandemic forces complete closure of schools during March-April 2022, but Term I exams are held at schools or centres.

Results would be based on the performance of students on Term I MCQ based examination and internal assessments. The weightage of marks of Term I examination conducted by the Board will be increased to provide year end results of candidates.

D. In case the situation of the pandemic forces complete closure of schools and Board conducted Term I and II exams are taken by the candidates from home in the session 2021-22.

Results would be computed on the basis of the Internal Assessment/Practical/Project Work and Theory marks of Term-I and II exams taken by the candidate from home in Class X / XII subject to the moderation or other measures to ensure validity and reliability of the assessment.

In all the above cases, data analysis of marks of students will be undertaken to ensure the integrity of internal assessments and home based exams.

Dr. Joseph Emmanuel
Director (Academics)

CHAPTER 01

Internet Basics

In this Chapter...

- History of Internet
- Working of Internet
- Connecting to the Internet
- World Wide Web (WWW)
- Web Browser, Web Client and Web Server
- Web Address/URL
- Domain Name
- E-mail Address
- Blogs and Newsgroup
- Internet Protocols

The term Internet is derived from the words 'interconnection' and 'networks'. A network is a collection of two or more computers, which are connected together to share information and resources.

The Internet is a worldwide system of computer networks, i.e. **network of networks**. Through Internet, computers become able to exchange information with each other and find diverse perspective on issues from a global audience. Most of the people uses Internet for sending and receiving E-mail and net surfing for retrieving information.

Network of networks

History of Internet

In 1969, the University of California at Los Angeles and the University of Utah were connected with the beginning of the **ARPANET** (Advanced Research Projects Agency NETwork)

using 56 kbit/s circuits, which is sponsored by U.S. (United States) Department of Defense (DoD).

In mid 80's another federal agency, the National Science Foundation (NSF) created a new high capacity network called **NSFnet** (National Science Foundation network), which was more capable than ARPANET.

Several private organisations and people started working to build their own networks, named **private networks**, which were later (in 1990's) connected with ARPANET and NSFnet to form the **Internet**. The Internet really became popular in 1990's after the development of World Wide Web (WWW).

Working of Internet

The computers on the Internet are connected to each other through small networks. These networks are connected through the gateways to the Internet backbone.

All computers on the Internet, communicate with one another using TCP/IP, which is a basic protocol of the Internet.

TCP/IP (Transmission Control Protocol/Internet Protocol) manages the transmission of data/file/document on the Internet by breaking the data/file/document into small pieces or parts called **packets** or **datagrams**.

Each packet contains actual data and address part, i.e. addresses of destination and source upto 1500 characters.

Functioning of TCP and IP are as follows

- **TCP** It breaks message into smaller packets that are transmitted over the Internet and also reassembles these smaller packets into the original message that are received from the Internet.
- **IP** It handles the address part of each packet, so that the data is sent to the correct address. Each gateway on the network check this address to see where to forward the message.

Uses of Internet

Internet has been the most useful technology of the modern time, which helps us not only in our daily lives, but also in our personal and professional lives developments.

Thus, some uses of Internet are as follows

- E-Commerce (auction, buying and selling products, etc.)
- Research (online journals, magazines, information, etc.)
- Education (E-learning, distance learning, etc.)
- E-Governance (online filling of application, Income Tax, Sales Tax, etc.)
- E-Reservation (online reservation, online ticket booking, etc.)
- Online Payments (credit and debit card payments, etc.)
- Video Conferencing
- Exchange of Views (files, music, folders, etc.)
- Social Networking Sites (facebook, twitter, etc.)
- Entertainment (play music, video games, etc.)

Advantages of Internet

There are some advantages, which are as follows

(i) Greater access to information reduces research time.

(ii) Allows you to easily communicate with other people.

(iii) Global reach enables one to connect everyone on the Internet.

(iv) Publishing documents on the Internet saves paper.

(v) A valuable resource for companies to advertise and conduct business.

Disadvantages of Internet

Although the Internet has various benefits and is one of the most powerful creations, it also contains many disadvantages. Below is given a list of the complete disadvantages of the Internet.

(i) Cyber frauds may take place involving credit/debit card numbers and details.

(ii) Unsuitable and undesirable material is available that sometimes can be used by notorious people such as terrorists.

(iii) It is a major source of computer viruses.

(iv) Messages sent across the Internet can be easily intercepted and are open to abuse by others.

(v) It is difficult to check the accuracy of information available on the Internet.

Connecting to the Internet

There are mainly three ways of connecting to the Internet, which are as follows

1. Dial-up Connection

It is a temporary connection, set-up between your computer and ISP server. Dial-up connection uses the telephone line (Public Switched Telephone Network-PSTN) and modem to connect to the Internet.

The modem connects the computer through the standard phone lines, which serves as the data transfer medium.

When a user initiates a dial-up connection, user needs to enter the password and specify a username and modem dials a phone number of an Internet Service Provider (ISP) that is designated to receive dial-up calls.

The ISP then establishes the connection, which usually takes about 10 sec and is accompanied by several beeping and buzzing sounds.

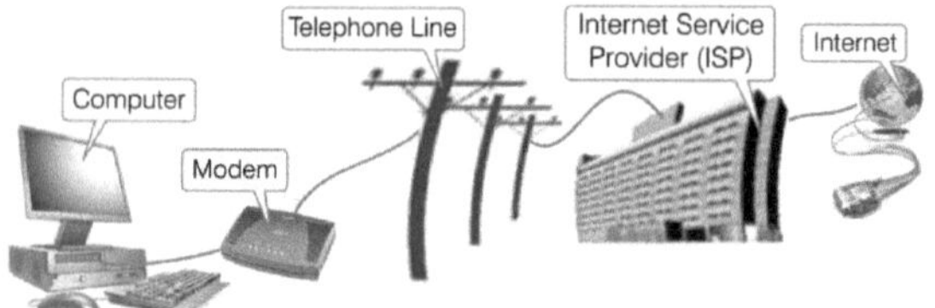

Dial-up connection

2. Broadband Connection

The term broadband commonly refers to high speed Internet access that is always ON and faster than the traditional dial-up access.

It is the short form of broadband width, that uses a telephone line to connect to the Internet. Speed of broadband connection is measured in Mbps (Megabits per second).

Broadband access allows users to connect to the Internet at greater speed than a standard 256 Kbps (Kilobits per second) modem or dial-up access. Broadband access requires the use of a broadband modem. Broadband includes several high speed transmission technologies, which are as follows

Digital Subscriber Line (DSL)

It is a popular broadband connection which provides Internet access by transmitting digital data over the wires of a local telephone network. It uses the existing copper telephone lines for Internet access.

A special modem is necessary in order to be able to use a DSL service over a standard phone line.

The several versions of DSL technique available today are as follows

- High Data rate DSL (HDSL)
- Very High Data rate DSL (VHDSL or VDSL)
- Asymmetrical DSL (ADSL)
- Symmetrical DSL (SDSL)
- Rate adaptive DSL (RDSL)
- ISDN DSL (IDSL)

Cable Modem

This service enables cable operators to provide broadband using the same co-axial cables, that deliver pictures and sound to your TV set. A cable modem can be added to or integrated with a set-top box that provides your TV set for Internet access. They provide transmission speed of 1.5 Mbps or more.

Broadband over Power Line (BPL)

It is the delivery of broadband over the existing low and medium voltage electric power distribution network. BPL can be provided to homes using existing electrical connections and outlets. It is also known as **power-band**.

BPL is good for those areas where there are no broadband connections, but power infrastructure exists. e.g. in rural areas.

3. Wireless Connection

Wireless broadband connects a home or business to the Internet using a radio link between the customer's location and the service provider's facility. Wireless broadband can be mobile or fixed.

Some ways to connect the Internet wirelessly are as follows

Wireless Fidelity (Wi-Fi)

It is a universal wireless networking technology that utilises radio frequencies to transfer data.

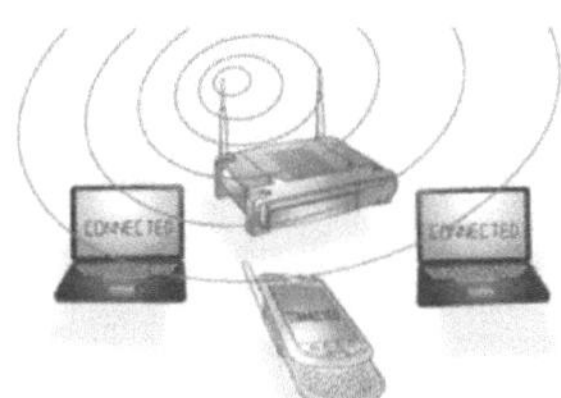

Wi-Fi network

Wi-Fi networks can be designed for private access within a home or business. It can be used for public Internet access at 'hot spots' that offers Wi-Fi access such as restaurants, coffee shops, hotels, airports, convention centres and city parks.

Worldwide Interoperability for Microwave Access (WiMAX)

These systems are expected to deliver Broadband Wireless Access (BWA) services upto 31 miles (45 km) for fixed stations and 3-10 miles (5-15 km) for mobile stations. WiMAX would

operate similar to Wi-Fi but at higher speed, over greater distances and for a greater number of users.

It has the ability to provide services even in areas that are difficult for wired infrastructure to reach.

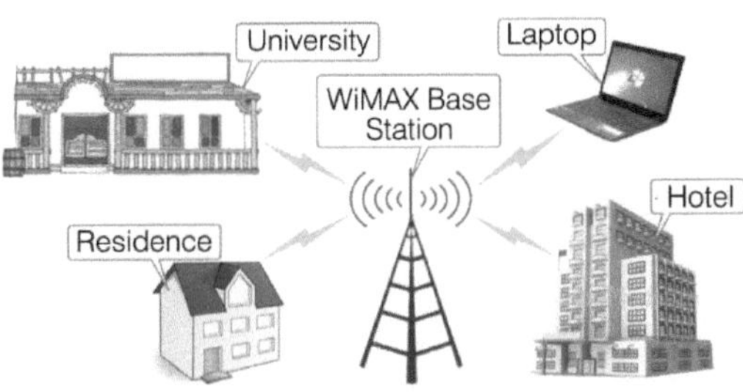

WiMAX network

Long Term Evolution (LTE)

It is a high-speed wireless broadband technology designed to support roaming Internet access by cell phones and handheld devices.

LTE is designed to allow upto 300 Mbps download and upto 75 Mbps upload with latency as low as 5 milliseconds. LTE works on multiple frequency bands often varying by country.

Note *Satellites which are orbiting around the earth, provide necessary links for telephone and television service, can also provide links for broadband.*

World Wide Web (WWW)

WWW was introduced on 13th March, 1989 by Tim Berners-Lee. It is a system of Internet servers that supports hypertext and multimedia to access several Internet protocols on a single interface. It is often abbreviated as the web or WWW or W3.

It is a way of exchanging information between computers on the Internet, trying to tie them together into a vast collection of interactive multimedia resources.

WWW Attributes

WWW provides various attributes, which are as follows

(i) **User-friendly** The WWW resource works smoothly with most web browsers, such as Internet Explorer, Firefox etc.

(ii) **Multimedia documents** WWW allows users to create and display web pages that contains various graphics, audio, video, animation and text.

(iii) **Interactive** WWW provides interactivity using hyperlinks and input boxes (i.e. textboxes and checkboxes).

(iv) **Frames** WWW supports frames that allow users to display more than one independent section on a single web page.

Web Page

The backbone of the World Wide Web is made up of files or documents called **pages** or **web pages**, that contain information and links to resources both text and multimedia.

CBSE Web page

It is created using HTML. The web is a collection of large number of computer documents and web pages that stored on computers around the world which are connected to one another using hyperlinks.

Website

A group of related web pages that follow the same theme and are connected together with hyperlinks is called a **website**.

A website displays related information on a specific topic. Each website is accessed by its own address known as URL (Uniform Resource Locator).

e.g. http://www.carwale.com is a website, while http://www.carwale.com/new/ is a web page.

Two terms that are associated with a website are as follows

Home Page

The main or first page of a website is known as home page.

The advantages of home page are as follows

(i) It helps viewers to find out what they can find on that particular site.

(ii) It helps in the publicity of an individual or a community.

(iii) It makes the visitors more comfortable with the website.

Web Portal

It is a specially designed website that often serves as the single point of access for information. It also has hyperlinks to many other websites.

The advantages of web portal are as follows

(i) Easy for users to customise personal places.

(ii) It provides communication between portals (i.e. different applications).

(iii) It provides flexible content and layout.

Web Browser

It is a software application that is used to locate, retrieve and display some content on the WWW, including web pages.

It is an interface that helps a computer user to gain access over all the content on the Internet. We can install more than one web browsers on a single computer. The user can navigate files, folders and websites with the help of a browser.

There are two types of web browsers, which are as follows

(i) **Text Web Browser** A web browser that displays only text-based information is known as text web browser. e.g. Lynx.

(ii) **Graphical Web Browser** A web browser that supports both text and graphic information is known as graphical web browser.

The first graphical web browser was NCSA Mosaic.

e.g. Internet Explorer, Firefox, Netscape, Safari, Google Chrome, Opera.

Web Client

It describes a special program designed as a user interface, through which messages are sent to a 'web server'.

Web clients usually operate within a web browser window, although some are installed to a mobile or computer as downloadable software.

A web client contains two parts: dynamic web pages and the web browser. Dynamic web pages are produced by components that run in the web tier and a web browser delivers web pages received from the server.

Web client is also known as a thin client because it does not execute heavy-duty operations such as querying databases, performing complex business tasks or connecting legacy applications.

Web Server

It is a computer program that serves requested HTML pages or files from the web client. Every web server that is connected to the Internet is associated with a unique address, i.e. IP address.

Web server software generally requires a fairly robust operating system like Unix, Windows NT.

Currently, there are five major web servers commonly used for hosting websites as follows

Apache HTTP Server

It was developed by Apache Software Foundation. The Apache HTTP server is the most popular web hosting server in the world.

This software can be installed virtually on all operating systems including Windows, Linux, Mac OS X, UNIX etc. At present, 60% of server machines run on the Apache web server.

Internet Information Server (IIS)

It is a product of Microsoft and is considered to be a very high performance web hosting server.

It is easily administrable and integrated with the Windows platforms.

Lighttpd

This is a free web hosting server distributed under the BSD license.

Lighttpd and web servers are compatible with Windows, Linux, Mac OS X, Unix and Solaris operating systems.

Sun Java System Web Server

It is developed by Sun Microsystems. It is not an open source server. It supports Windows, Linux and Unix operating systems.

Sun Java also supports many different technologies, scripts and languages including PHP, PERL, ASP, ColdFusion, Python etc.

Jigsaw Server

This is a free open source server for website hosting that comes straight from the W3C.

The Jigsaw web hosting server is written in Java and supports both PHP (Personal Home Page) programs and CGI (Common Gateway Interface) scripts. It supports different platforms like Linux, Mac OS X, Windows, Unix, FreeBSD etc.

Web Address/URL

Web is a collection of documents (web pages) stored on computers around the world. Each web page has an address describing where it can be found. This address is known as **Web address** or **URL (Uniform Resource Locator)**.

A web address identifies the location of a specific web page on the Internet, such as

http://www.learnyoga.com

Every computer connected to the Internet has its unique web address, without which it cannot be reached by other computers.

Parts of URL

The URL contains three parts, which are as follows

(i) The name of the protocol to be used to access the file resource.

(ii) A domain name that identifies a specific computer on the Internet.

(iii) A path name with hierarchical description that specifies the location of a file in that computer.

e.g.

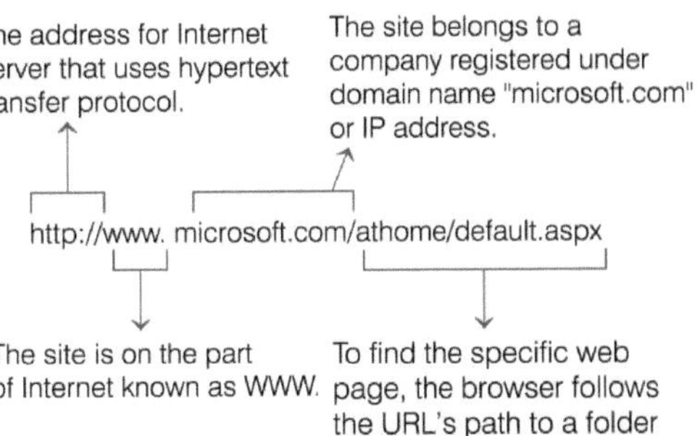

Types of URL

URLs fall into two categories

(i) **Absolute URL** It specifies the exact location of a file/directory on the Internet. Absolute URL identifies that each URL is unique, which means that if two URLs are identical then they point to the same file.

(ii) **Relative URL** It points to a file/directory in relation to the present file/directory. It locates a resource using an absolute URL as a starting point. It typically consists of the path and optionally, the resource but no scheme or no server.

Domain Name

It is the text name corresponding to the numeric IP address of a computer on the Internet. Internet users access your website using your domain name.

It is a way to identify and locate computers connected to the Internet. It must be unique. Domain name always have two or more parts, separated by periods (dots).

e.g. google.com, yahoo.com etc.

Domain Abbreviation

Domains are organised by the type of organisation and by the country.

A three letter abbreviation indicating the organisation and usually two letter abbreviation indicating the country name. Most common domain abbreviations for organisation are as follows:

info	Informational organisation
com	Commercial
gov	Government
edu	Education
mil	Military
net	Network resources
org	Usually non-profit organisation

Some domain abbreviations for country are as follows

in	India
au	Australia
fr	France
nz	New Zealand
uk	United Kingdom

Domain Name System (DNS)

It translates domain names (computers host names) into IP addresses. It also stores and associates many types of information with domain names.

DNS can be quickly updated and specifies the technical functionality of database service.

The naming scheme by which servers are identified is known as the domain name system. e.g. the domain name www.example.com might translate to 198.105.232.4.

E-mail Address

E-mail stands for 'Electronic Mail'. It is a paperless method of sending messages, notes, pictures and even sound files from one place to another using the Internet as a medium.

It is an individual name, which is used to send and receive E-mail on the Internet. It is used to specify the source or destination of an E-mail message.

The format of an E-mail address is username@domainname, where

- username identifies a unique user name.
- "@" separates the user from the domain name. Domain identifies the mail server.

e.g.

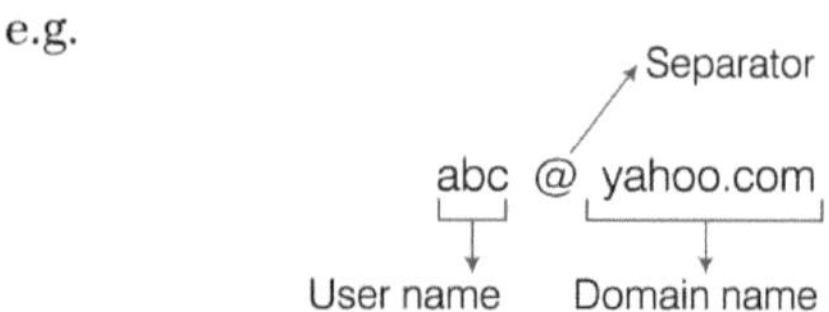

Some sites which provide the E-mail services are Gmail, Yahoo! mail, Rediffmail etc.

Blogs

A blog is a website or a web page, in which an individual records opinion links to other sites on regular basis. A blog content is written frequently and added in a chronological order. It is written online and visible to everyone.

In education, blogs can be used as instructional resources. These blogs are referred to as **edublogs**. The entries of blog are also known as **posts**.

A person who writes a blog or a weblog is known as **blogger**. Blogging is the act of posting content on a blog.

Blogs are fall into various categories: Personal blog, News and views, Company blogs and Micro-blogs.

Advantages of Blogs

There are some advantages, which are as follows

  (i) You can work at any time of the day and work with your ease.

  (ii) Blogger does not require more efforts to write articles for his/her blog.

  (iii) Easy and quick to update or add new posts.

  (iv) People can leave comments on your blog.

  (v) It increases blog revenue.

  (vi) Blogs can be set-up quickly.

  (vii) It is all about being social. You (blogger) need to answer to peoples' queries and for that, reading should be a part of day-to-day tasks.

Disadvantages of Blogs

There are some disadvantages, which are as follows

  (i) The common problem of full time blogger is isolation from society.

  (ii) Mostly people love blogging but they don't have a fix source of income. Some choose freelance writing job for earning money and few chooses to depend on their parents to fulfil the need of money.

  (iii) If the blogger get ill, then they don't get time to update their blog and it ultimately results in loss of blog income and traffic.

Newsgroup

An area on a computer network especially the Internet, devoted to the discussion of a specified topic is known as Newsgroup.

It is an online discussion group that allows interaction through electronic bulletin board system (Usenet) and chat sessions.

Newsgroup and contents are stored on special servers called **Network News Transfer Protocol** (NNTP) servers. The groups can be either "moderated", where a person or group decides which postings will become part of the discussion or "unmoderated", where everything posted is included in the discussion.

Advantages of Newsgroup

The advantages of newsgroup are as follows

  (i) Newsgroup is similar in some ways to mailing lists, but it has a better structure.

  (ii) It is also easier to access a newsgroup.

  (iii) Usually, you will be able to find a FAQ (Frequently Asked Questions) section on a newsgroup, which is always helpful for those who are not sure of certain things.

  (iv) Free to subscribe and post.

Disadvantages of Newsgroup

The disadvantages of newsgroup are as follows

  (i) A newsgroup is not as quick as an E-mail or even a mailing list.

  (ii) The information on newsgroup is submitted by people who may have no real idea of what they are talking about.

  (iii) It is not user friendly and the risk of viruses is high.

Internet Protocols

Protocol refers to the set of rules applicable for a network. Many different types of network protocols and standards are required to ensure that your computer can communicate with another computer located on the next desk or half-way around the world.

In a computer network, a protocol allows the setting up of a valid connection, communication and data transferring between two computing end points or computer system.

Some of the commonly used protocols are as follows

TCP/IP (Transmission Control Protocol/Internet Protocol)

TCP/IP defines the rules, computers must follow to communicate with each other over the Internet.

The TCP is a protocol which is responsible for finding path for the destination. It also splits the message into several datagrams, if it does not fit in one datagram.

IP (Internet Protocol) used by the Internet for transferring messages from one machine to another. The messages are sent in the form of packets. IP defines the packet structures that encapsulate the data to be delivered.

SMTP (Simple Mail Transfer Protocol)

SMTP is the standard protocol for E-mail services on a TCP/IP network. SMTP provides the ability to send and receive E-mail messages.

The SMTP standard defines the conversation between the sender of an E-mail and the SMTP mail server that delivers the mail. In a SMTP conversation, the sender issues a certain sequence of commands to the receiving SMTP server.

Generally, if the sender issues valid commands and the intended recipients of the E-mail are valid accounts on the receiving server, the receiving server will accept the message and attempt to deliver it.

POP3 (Post Office Protocol version 3)

It is a standard mail protocol used to receive E-mails from a remote server to a local email client. POP3 allows you to download E-mail messages on your local computer and read them even when you are offline.

When you use POP3 to connect to your E-mail account, messages are downloaded locally and removed from the E-mail server. This means that if you access your account from multiple locations, that may not be the best option for you.

HTTP (HyperText Transfer Protocol)

HTTP is an application level protocol. This protocol is used by the world wide web. HTTP defines how messages are formatted and transmitted and what actions web servers and browsers should take in response to various commands.

It is a stateless protocol because each command is executed independently without any knowledge of the commands that came before it.

HTTPS

HTTPS is a secure version of HyperText Transfer Protocol. It is the primary protocol used to send data between a web browser and a website.

The use of HTTPS protects against eavesdropping and man-in-the-middle attacks.

This is particularly important when users transmit sensitive data, such as by logging into a bank account, E-mail service or health insurance provider.

HTTP vs HTTPS

The differences between HTTP and HTTPS are as follows

HTTP	HTTPS
It is used for unsecured communication over Internet.	HTTPS is used for secured communication over computer network used as Internet.
Do not use any security protocols.	It uses security protocols at transport layer SSL/TSL and also at layer-2 and layer-3.
e.g. Websites like Internet forums, educational sites.	e.g. Websites like banking websites, payment gateway, shopping websites, etc.

Remote Login and File Transfer Protocols

A remote login is a technique to create connection with a remote computer.

Remote file transfer is the process of transferring or sending a file to a device or network node external to the local network.

Some protocols are used for this purpose as follows

FTP (File Transfer Protocol)

It is a standard network protocol used to transfer files from one host to another host over a TCP-based network, such as the Internet.

FTP is based on client/server principle. It establishes two connections between the hosts. One connection is used for data transfer, which is opened and closed for each file transfer and the other for control information, which remains connected during the entire interactive FTP session.

Remote Login (Telnet)

Telnet is a protocol used for creating a connection with a remote computer. Once your telnet client establishes a connection to the remote host, telnet client becomes a virtual terminal, allowing you to communicate with the remote host from your computer.

It establishes a connection either with command line client or with a programmatic interface. Telnet provides an error free connection, which is always faster than the latest conventional modems.

SSH (Secure Shell)

The SSH protocol is a method for secure remote login from one computer to another. It provides several alternative options for strong authentication and it protects the communications security and integrity with strong encryption.

SFTP (Secure File Transfer Protocol)

SFTP, also called SSH File Transfer Protocol, is a network protocol for accessing, transferring and managing files on remote systems.

It allows businesses to securely transfer billing data, funds and data recovery files.

SCP (Secure Copy)

It is a file transfer protocol, which helps in transferring computer files securely from a local host to a remote host. It works on the Secure Shell (SSH) protocol technique.

Terms Related to Internet

- **HTML** (HyperText Markup Language) It is a markup language used for designing web pages. A markup language is a set of markup (angular bracket, < >) tags, which tell the web browser, how to display a Web page's words and images for the user.
- A **modem** changes the digital data into analog data and *vice-versa* at source computer in a format that can be carried by telephone lines. Modem stands for Modulator and Demodulator.
- **Bandwidth** is the amount of data that a circuit or a signal can carry.
- **ISDN** (Integrated Services Digital Network) establishes the connection using the phone lines which carry digital signals instead of analog signals.
- **ISP** (Internet Service Provider) refers to the companies that provide Internet connections to the users.

  Some popular ISPs of India are:
  - Data Communication Ltd.
  - Mahanagar Telephone Nigam Ltd. (MTNL)
  - Airtel
  - Reliance
- **HyperText and Hyperlinks** HyperText is the text that appears on the page, on which we can click and reach to another page with which it is linked. HyperText is also a combination of hyperlinks and multimedia. Hyperlink or dynamic link simply called a link, may be an icon, graphic or text in a document that links to another document.
- **Intranet** is a collection of private computer networks within an organisation. It is also known as **corporate portal** or **private business network.**
- **Extranet** refers to network within an organisation, using Internet to connect to the outsiders in controlled manner.
- **Numeric Computer IP Address** IP addresses are in aaa.aaa.aaa.aaa format, where each aaa is a number from 0 to 255. The length of IP address is 4 bytes. IP addresses identify the host computers, so that packets of information reached to the correct computer.

  e.g. 162.192.1.89

Chapter Practice

Objective Questions

• Multiple Choice Questions

1. What can you do with the Internet? **[CBSE 2011]**
(a) Exchange information with friends and colleagues.
(b) Access pictures, sounds, video clips and other media elements.
(c) Find diverse perspective on issues from a global audience.
(d) Exchange information, access pictures, find diverse perspective on issue from a global audience.

Ans. (d) Internet is a world wide system of computer networks that exchanges information, access pictures, find diverse perspective on issues from a global audience.

2. The first network was
(a) ARPANET
(b) Internet
(c) NSFnet
(d) NET

Ans. (a) The Advanced Research Projects Agency NETwork (ARPANET) was the world's first operational packet switching network.

3. Which communication protocol is used by Internet?
(a) TCP/IP   (b) WWW   (c) HTML   (d) W3C

Ans. (a) TCP/IP (Transmission Control Protocol/Internet Protocol) is a communication protocol used by Internet which manages the transmission of data/file document on the Internet.

4. In Internet Protocol (IP), data is organised in the form of
(a) bundles
(b) packets
(c) switches
(d) parts

Ans. (b) IP is used by Internet for transferring messages from one machine to another. In Internet Protocol (IP), data is organised in the form of packets.

5. Digital information is converted into analog information by the modem at **[CBSE 2011]**
(a) destination computer
(b) source computer
(c) Both (a) and (b)
(d) Neither (a) nor (b)

Ans. (b) Digital information is converted into analog information by modem at source computer. While, analog information is converted into digital information at destination computer.

6. An organisation responsibles for providing Internet services to customer is commonly known as
(a) government
(b) ISP
(c) TCP/IP
(d) HTTP

Ans. (b) An organisation responsibles for providing Internet services to customer is commonly known as ISP (Internet Service Provider). It registers themselves under the government domain according to the copyright law.

7. Which of these services will not be provided by a typical Internet Service Provider (ISP)?
(a) An E-mail address
(b) Modem
(c) A connection to the Internet
(d) Technical help

Ans. (a) ISP refers to a company that provides Internet services, modem, connection and technical help. It does not provide an E-mail address.

8. Nick connects to the Internet at home using a laptop computer with a wireless connection. Nick is going to change to a desktop computer using a 1 Gbps ethernet cable connection.
Which of these should be the result of making the changes?
(a) Increased portability and decreased speed.
(b) Decreased portability and increased speed.
(c) Increased portability and increased speed.
(d) Decreased portability and decreased speed.

Ans. (b) Decreased portability and increased speed will be the result.

9. Combination of multimedia and hyperlink is called
(a) hypermedia
(b) E-mail
(c) hypertext
(d) None of the above

Ans. (c) Hypertext refers to the combination of text, graphic images, audio and video tracks and hyperlinks.

10. On Internet, to go to other web page through button, the user should use **[CBSE 2012]**
(a) search tools (b) find and replace
(c) search engine (d) hyperlink

Ans. (d) On Internet, to go to other web page available through button, the user should use hyperlinks. These hyperlinks may be an icon, graphics or text.

11. A collection of web pages linked together in a random order is **[CBSE 2014]**
(a) a website (b) a web server
(c) a search engine (d) a web browser

Ans. (a) A website is a collection of web pages linked together in a random order and displays related information on a specific topic.

12. Home page helps viewers to find out what they can find on the particular site. Home page is the
(a) first page of a website (b) index page
(c) about page (d) None of these

Ans. (a) Home page refers to the initial or main or first web page of a website, sometimes called the front page. It helps viewers to find out what they can find on the particular site.

13. Which of the following is/are a popular web browser? **[CBSE 2019]**
(a) Firefox (b) Safari
(c) Navigator (d) All of these

Ans. (d) Web browser is a software application that is used to locate, retrieve and display some content on the WWW. Firefox, Safari, Navigator all are popular web browsers.

14. Google Chrome is an example of
(a) web browser (b) web server
(c) HTTP (d) WWW

Ans. (a) Web browser is the program that is used to explore the Internet. Thus, Google Chrome is an example of web browser.

15. A web page is located using a
(a) Universal Record Linking
(b) Uniform Resource Locator
(c) Universal Record Locator
(d) Uniformly Reachable Links

Ans. (b) URL (Uniform Resource Locator) specifies the location of a specific web page on the Internet.

16. In URL, http://www.arihant.com/index.htm, which component identifies the path of a web page?
(a) http
(b) www.arihant.com
(c) /index.htm
(d) All of the above

Ans. (c) /index.htm, because path name identifies the path of a web page.

17. Kirti, a student, has written some points about web pages and URL. **[CBSE 2015]**
(i) Which of the following statements are true about web pages?
(a) You cannot E-mail a link of web page.
(b) You cannot create a web page.
(c) Web pages are written in HTML.
(d) Web pages are viewed through browser.

(ii) Which of the following statements are true about URL?
(a) URL means Uniform Resource Locator.
(b) You can enter URL into address bar.
(c) An example of URL is we@fg.com.
(d) It is not necessary for URL to be unique.

Ans. (i) (c) and (d) (ii) (a) and (b)

18. Domain names always have two or more parts, separated by
(a) commas (b) periods (called dots)
(c) semicolon (d) None of these

Ans. (b) A domain name is a hierarchical series of character strings representing different levels of domains separated by dot/period.

19. In all computers on the Internet, owned and operated by education institution form part of the
(a) .com domain (b) .edu domain
(c) .mil domain (d) .org domain

Ans. (b) In all computers on the Internet, owned and operated by education institution form part of the .edu domain.

20. Each computer connected to the Internet must
(a) be a pentium machine
(b) have a unique IP address
(c) have a web browser
(d) have a modem connection

Ans. (b) Each computer connected to the Internet must have a unique IP address. IP addresses are in aaa.aaa.aaa.aaa format, where each aaa is a number from 0 to 255.

21. An IP address is a string of .... numbers separated by periods. **[CBSE 2011]**
(a) 3 (b) 4
(c) 2 (d) 5

Ans. (b) An IP address consists of 4 numbers separated by periods.

22. IP addresses are converted into **[CBSE 2013]**
(a) a binary string
(b) alphanumeric string
(c) a hierarchy of domain names
(d) a hexadecimal string

Ans. (c) IP addresses are converted into a hierarchy of domain names. DNS (Domain Name System) translates domain names into their IP addresses and *vice-versa*.

23. A blog consists of
(a) images
(b) text
(c) links
(d) All of these

Ans. (d) A blog is a website or a web page, in which an individual records opinion links to other sites on regular basis. A blog consists of images, text and links.

24. Online discussion through posts about various topics is called
(a) E-Discussion
(b) Newsgroup
(c) E-mail
(d) Chat

Ans. (b) Online discussion through posts about various topics is called newsgroup.

25. HTML is a markup language for describing web document. HTML uses
(a) pre-specified tags
(b) user defined tags
(c) tags only for linking
(d) fixed tags defined by the language

Ans. (d) HTML (HyperText Markup Language) is a markup language for describing web document. HTML uses fixed tags defined by the language.

26. A set of rules that governs data communication is
(a) protocol
(b) information
(c) HTML
(d) E-mail

Ans. (a) A protocol is a set of rules that governs the communication between computers on a network.

27. Which of the following would you use to transfer files over the Internet?
(a) FTP
(b) E-mail
(c) HTTP
(d) Browser

Ans. (a) FTP (File Transfer Protocol) is used to transfer files between computers on a network.

28. Full form of FTP is   [CBSE 2018]
(a) Force Transfer Protocol
(b) File Transport Protocol
(c) File Transmission Protocol
(d) File Transfer Protocol

Ans. (d) FTP stands for File Transfer Protocol. FTP is a protocol through which Internet users can upload files from their computer to a website.

• Case Based MCQs

Direction *Read the case and answer the following questions* .

29. It is a temporary connection, set-up between your computer and ISP server.

Dial-up connection uses the telephone line (PSTN) and modem to connect to the Internet. The modem connects the computer through the standard phone lines, which serves as the data transfer medium.

When a user initiates a dial-up connection, user needs to enter the password and specify a username and modem dials a phone number of an ISP, i.e. is designated to receive dial-up calls.

The ISP then establishes the connection, which usually takes about few seconds and its accompanied by several beeping and buzzing sounds.

(i) Which of the following uses telephone line to connect to the Internet?
(a) Dial-up (b) Bluetooth   (c) Wi-Fi   (d) WiMax

(ii) The full form of PSTN is
(a) Public Switched Target Network
(b) Public Switched Telephone Network
(c) Public Switched Telegram Network
(d) Public Switched Temporary Network

(iii) ISP is used for
(a) connecting your computer to printer
(b) connecting your computer to fax machine
(c) connecting your computer to the Internet
(d) None of the above

(iv) ISP stands for
(a) Internet Service Provider
(b) Internet Socket Provider
(c) Internet Service Publish
(d) Internet Standard Provider

(v) How many time taken by ISP to establish the connection?
(a) 15 sec
(b) 18 sec
(c) 20 sec
(d) 10 sec

Ans. (i) (a) Dial-up connection uses the telephone line (Public Switched Telephone Network–PSTN) and modem to connect to the Internet.

(ii) (b) The full form of PSTN is Public Switched Telephone Network. It is the world's collection of inter-connected voice-oriented public telephone networks.

(iii) (c) ISP is used for connecting your computer to the Internet.

(iv) (a) ISP stands for Internet Service Provider. It refers to the companies that provide Internet connections to the users.

(v) (d) The ISP then establishes the connection, which usually takes about 10 sec and its accompanied by several beeping and buzzing sounds.

30. For communication over the Internet, the communicating devices must follow certain rules. These rules are called Internet protocols. For E-mail communication, we use SMTP and POP. For communication between browser and server HTTP and HTTPS protocols are used. We can use

TELNET to access services available on a remote computer. **[Specimen Paper 2020]**

(i) Which of the following is an Internet protocol?
   (a) HTTP
   (b) FTP
   (c) Both (a) and (b)
   (d) None of these

(ii) SMTP protocol is
   (a) used for composing an E-mail message
   (b) used in receiving incoming E-mails by pulling the message from server to client
   (c) used in sending outgoing E-mails by pushing the message from client to server
   (d) None of the above

(iii) POP protocol is
   (a) used for composing an E-mail message
   (b) used in receiving incoming E-mails by pulling the message from server to client
   (c) used in sending outgoing E-mails by pushing the message from client to server
   (d) None of the above

(iv) Which of the following Internet Protocols (IPs) provides secure data transmission between server and browser with the help of encryption?
   (a) HTTP
   (b) HTTPS
   (c) TELNET
   (d) ARPANET

(v) The full form of POP (E-mail protocol) is
   (a) Post Order Protocol
   (b) Push Order Protocol
   (c) Post Office Protocol
   (d) Pull Over Protocol

(vi) Which of the following protocol is used for delivering data from the source to the destination?
   (a) TCP
   (b) IP
   (c) SMTP
   (d) ARPANET

(vii) The full form of SMTP is
   (a) Secure Mail Transfer Protocol
   (b) Secure Mail Transmit Protocol
   (c) Simple Mail Transmit Protocol
   (d) Simple Mail Transfer Protocol

Ans. (i) (c) Protocol refers to the set of rules applicable for a network. HTTP and FTP are Internet protocol in which HTTP is used by the world wide web while FTP is used to transfer files from one host to another host over Internet.

(ii) (c) SMTP protocol is used in sending outgoing E-mails by pushing the message from client to server.

(iii) (b) POP (Post Office Protocol) is used in receiving incoming E-mails by pulling the message from server to client.

(iv) (b) HTTPS is a secure version of HyperText Transfer Protocol. It provides secure data transmission between server and browser with the help of encryption.

(v) (c) The full form of POP is Post Office Protocol. It is a type of computer networking and Internet standard protocol that extracts and retrieves E-mail from a remote mail server for access by the host machine.

(vi) (b) IP (Internet Protocol) is used for delivering data from the source to the destination. It defines the packet structures that encapsulates the data to be delivered.

(vii) (d) The full form of SMTP is Simple Mail Transfer Protocol. It enables the transmission and delivery of E-mail over the Internet.

PART 2
Subjective Questions

• Short Answer Type Questions

1. Mention any two major uses of Internet. **[CBSE 2003]**

Ans. The two major uses of Internet are as follows
   (i) For the students and educational purposes, Internet is widely used to gather information so as to do the research.
   (ii) We can send/receive the mail all over the world.

2. How do Internet help us?

Ans. Internet can be useful for us in following ways
   (i) Allows organisations to advertise their products.
   (ii) Provides information.
   (iii) Easily communicate with other people.
   (iv) Save paper as we can publish documents on the Internet.

3. Write three disadvantages of using Internet.

Ans. The three disadvantages of using Internet are as follows
   (i) Cyber frauds
   (ii) Information misuse
   (iii) Computer virus circulation

4. What is MODEM? **[CBSE 2006]**

Ans. MODEM stands for MOdulator/DEModulator. It is a hardware device that enables a computer to send and receive information over telephone lines by converting the digital data used by your computer into an analog signal used on telephone lines and then converting back once received on the other end.

5. Define home page. Give two advantages of home page.

Ans. A home page is the first page of a website.
   Two advantages of home page are as follows
   (i) It helps viewers to find out what they can find on that site.
   (ii) Publicity of an individual or a community.

6. Many organisations use both Internet and Intranet. Give some differences between Internet and Intranet.

Ans. Differences between Internet and Intranet are as follows

(i) Internet is a Wide Area Network (WAN), while Intranet is a Local Area Network (LAN).

(ii) Greater amount of information is available on Internet, while on Intranet specific amount of information is available.

(iii) Internet is not safe as Intranet can be safely privatised as per the need.

7. Write a short note on IP address and give its characteristics.

Ans. Internet internally follows number based addressing system. Numeric address of a computer is called IP address by a scheme called Domain Name System (DNS). The IP address consists of four numbers from 0 to 255, separated by dots.

The characteristics of an IP address are as follows

(i) IP addresses are unique.

(ii) IP addresses are global and standardised.

8. How do you differentiate between a web address and an E-mail address? **[CBSE 2018]**

Ans. The basic differences between a web address and an E-mail address are as follows

(i) E-mail address is a network address whereas web address is the Internet address.

(ii) An E-mail address always contains the 'at the rate' sign (@) whereas, a web address never does.

9. Discuss the role of web servers and web clients briefly. **[CBSE 2019]**

Ans. **Web server** is a computer program that serves requested HTML pages or files from the web client. Every web server that is connected to the Internet is associated with a unique address, i.e. IP address.

Web client is a computing term which describes special program designed as a user interface, through which messages are sent to a web server.

10. What is the significance of HTTP?

Ans. HTTP is a protocol used on Internet. It works in combination with WWW. It allows us to access hypertext documents on WWW. Since, WWW allows us to access or use multimedia files on the Internet and the hypertext files support multimedia.

11. What is digital subscriber line?

Ans. Digital Subscriber Line (DSL) is a popular broadband connection which provides Internet access by transmitting digital data over the wires of a local telephone network. It uses the existing copper telephone lines for Internet access. A special modem is necessary in order to be able to use a DSL service over a standard phone line.

12. What are the types of URL?

Ans. URLs vary depending on the location of the document to which user will link.

Basically, URLs fall into two categories

(i) **Absolute URL** It specifies the exact location of a file/directory on the Internet. Absolute URL identifies that each URL is unique, which means that if two URLs are identical then they point to the same file.

(ii) **Relative URL** It points to a file/directory in relation to the present file/directory. It locates a resource using an absolute URL as a starting point. It typically consists of the path and optionally, the resource but no scheme or no server.

13. Write the web extensions (top level domain names) given to a websites of the following types of organisations.

(i) educational

(ii) government

(iii) network organisation

(iv) commercial

Ans. (i) .edu   (ii) .gov

(iii) .net   (iv) .com

14. Distinguish between FTP and Telnet.

Ans. The differences between FTP and Telent are as follows

FTP	Telnet
FTP stands for File Transfer Protocol.	Telenet stands for Telecommunication Network.
FTP is used for downloading the files.	Telnet is also used for chat operation.
It establishes two connections, one is for control command and another is for data transfer.	It uses only one connection.

15. Mr. Lal owns a factory which manufactures automobile spare parts. Tell him about the web page and also suggest the advantages of having a web page for this factory.

Ans. The backbone of the World Wide Web is made up of files or documents called web pages, that contains information and links to resources both text and multimedia.

The web page provides the information to the clients about his factory of spare parts. Moreover, he can receive the order on the Internet from the clients using the web page.

16. What is WWW? **[CBSE 2018]**

Ans. WWW (World Wide Web) is a system of Internet servers that supports hypertext and multimedia to access several Internet protocols on a single interface.

17. What do you understand by remote login?

Ans. Remote login is a process in which user can login into remote site i.e. computer and use services that are available on the remote computer. With the help of remote login a user is able to understand result of transferring, result of processing from the remote computer to the local computer.

18. What is the full form of URL ?

Or What is URL ? **[CBSE 2019]**

Ans. URL stands for Uniform Resource Locator, which is simply an address of a document on the web, more accurately, on the Internet. It specifies the Internet address of a file stored on a host computer connected to the Internet.

19. Write a short note on HTML.

Ans. HTML is a markup language used for designing web pages. A markup language is a set of markup (angular bracket, < >) tags, which tell the web browser, how to display a web page's words and images for the user.

20. Can we use URL to access a web page? How ?

Ans. Yes, we can use URL to access a web page, as a location on a web server, which is called a website and each website has a unique address known as URL.

21. Sarvesh, a student of Class X, is not able to understand the difference between web client and web server. Help him in understanding the same by explaining their role and giving suitable example of each. **[Specimen Paper 2020]**

Ans. Differences between web client and web server are as follows

Web client	Web server
It is an application that communicates with a web server, using HyperText Transfer Protocol (HTTP).	It is a piece of software designed to serve web pages/websites/web services.
e.g. web browser.	e.g. IIS, Apache and many more.

22. Define Internet and write its two uses in our daily life. How is it different from the World Wide Web (WWW). **[Specimen Paper 2020]**

Ans. Internet is a world wide system of computer networks, i.e. network of networks. Through Internet, computers become able to exchange information with each other and find diverse perspective on issues from a global audience.

Two uses of Internet are as follows

(i) E-commerce (auction, buying and selling products).

(ii) Social networking sites (facebook, twitter, etc).

Difference between www and Internet is

WWW It is just a common point of connectivity for information sharing that is facilitated by a global network of computers.

Internet It is a connection between computers and countless other devices that form a huge network of systems.

• Long Answer Type Questions

23. Why is Internet called 'Network of Networks'?

Ans. Internet is called 'Network of Networks' because it is global network of computers that are linked together by cables and telephone lines making communication possible among them. It can be defined as a global network over a million of smaller heterogeneous computer networks. The network which consists of thousands of networks spanning the entire globe is known as Internet. The Internet is a world wide collection of networked computers, which are able to exchange information with each other very quickly.

Mostly people use the Internet in two ways, E-mail and World Wide Web. In Internet, most computers are not connected directly, they are connected to smaller networks, which in turn are connected through gateways to the Internet backbone. A gateway is a device that connects dissimilar networks. A backbone is central interconnecting structure that connects one or more networks.

24. What is DNS and also explain its functions? **[CBSE 2013]**

Ans. DNS stands for Domain Name System. It is a hierarchical distributed naming system for computers, services or any resources connected to the Internet or a private network. It associates various information with domain names assigned to each of the participating entities.

The different functions of DNS are as follows

(i) It translates meaningful domain names into the numerical IP addresses, which is needed for the purpose of locating computer services and devices world wide.

(ii) It serves as the phone book for the Internet by translating human friendly computer host names into IP addresses.

(iii) The DNS can be quickly updated, allowing a service's location on the network to change without affecting the end users.

(iv) It distributes the responsibility of assigning domain names and mapping those names to IP addresses by designating authoritative names servers for each domain.

(v) It also specifies the technical functionality of database service. It defines the DNS protocol, a detailed specification of the data structure and data communication exchanges used in DNS, as part of the Internet Protocol Suite (IPS).

25. How did the Internet begin?

Ans. In 1969, the University of California at Los Angeles and the University of Utah were connected with the beginning of the ARPANET (Advanced Research Projects Agency NETwork) using 56 kbit/s circuits, which is sponsored by U.S. (United States) Department of Defense (DoD). The goal of this project was to connect computers at different Universities and U.S. defense.

In mid 80's another federal agency, the National Science Foundation (NSF) created a new high capacity network called NSFnet (National Science Foundation network), which was more capable than ARPANET. The only drawback of NSFnet was that it allowed only academic research on its network and not any kind of private business on it.

Now, several private organisations and people started working to build their own networks, named private networks, which were later (in 1990's) connected with ARPANET and NSFnet to form the Internet. The Internet really became popular in 1990's after the development of World Wide Web (WWW).

26. Explain some popular graphical web browsers.

Ans. Some popular graphical web browsers are as follows

  (i) **Netscape** It was introduced in 1994. Netscape comprises the major portion of the browser's market.

  (ii) **Internet Explorer** (IE) It is a product of Microsoft. This is the most commonly used browser in the world. This was introduced in 1995 alongwith Windows 95 launch and it has passed Netscape popularity in 1998.

  (iii) **Firefox** It is a new browser derived from Mozilla. It was initially released in 2002 and has grown to be the second most popular browser on the Internet.

  (iv) **Safari** It is a web browser developed by Apple Incorporation and included in Mac OS X. It was first released as a public beta in January 2003. Safari provides good support for latest technologies like XHTML, CSS2 etc.

  (v) **Google Chrome** This web browser was developed by Google. Its beta and commercial version was released in September 2008 for Microsoft Windows.

  (vi) **Opera** It was initially released in 1995. It is smaller and faster than most other browsers, yet it is fully featured. It is the most popular mobile web browser.

27. Which protocol is the communication protocol for the Internet? Also, explain this protocol.

Ans. TCP/IP is the communication protocol for the Internet. It defines the rules, computers must follow to communicate with each other over the Internet. The TCP/IP is a protocol used with E-mail transmission. Infact, it is a set of protocol, i.e. TCP and IP.

TCP is a protocol, which is responsible for finding path for the destination. It also splits the message into several datagrams, if it does not fit in one datagram. Therefore, these datagrams are sent through different alternate paths towards the destination. The TCP makes sure that the datagram arrives at the destination correctly.

IP (**Internet Protocol**) used by the Internet for transferring messages from one machine to another. The messages are sent in the form of packets. IP defines the packet structures that encapsulate the data to be delivered. It also defines addressing methods that are used to label the datagram with source and destination format.

28. Write a detailed note on working of Internet.

Ans. The computers on the Internet are connected to each other through small networks. These networks are connected through the gateways to the Internet backbone.

All computers on the Internet, communicate with one another using TCP/IP, which is a basic protocol of the Internet.

TCP/IP (Transmission Control Protocol/Internet Protocol) manages the transmission of data/file/document on the Internet by breaking the data/file/document into small pieces or parts called **packets** or **datagrams**.

Each packet contains actual data and address part, i.e. addresses of destination and source upto 1500 characters.

Functioning of TCP and IP are as follows

TCP It breaks message into smaller packets that are transmitted over the Internet and also reassembles these smaller packets into the original message that are received from the Internet.

IP It handles the address part of each packet, so that the data is sent to the correct address. Each gateway on the network check this address to see where to forward the message.

29. Based on the paragraph, answer the questions that follow.

WWW was introduced on 13th March, 1989 by Tim Berners-Lee. It is a system of Internet servers that supports hypertext and multimedia to access several Internet protocols on a single interface. It is often abbreviated as the web or WWW or W3. It is a way of exchanging information between computers on the Internet, trying to tie them together into a vast collection of interactive multimedia resources. It is only a portion of what makes up the Internet, but it is the fastest growing part of the Internet.

The web lets people, organisations and companies publish information for other people to see. This makes the web a very useful tool for finding information about any topic.

  (i) What is WWW?

  (ii) What can a user do with WWW?

  (iii) Define the attributes that are provided by WWW.

Ans. (i) WWW (World Wide Web) is a system of Internet servers that supports hypertext and multimedia to access several, internet protocols on a single interface.

(ii) Using WWW, a user can download files, listen to music, view video files and jump to other documents or websites by using hypertext links.

(iii) WWW provides various attributes, which are as follows

    (a) **User-friendly** The WWW resource works smoothly with most web browsers, such as Internet Explorer, Firefox etc.

    (b) **Multimedia documents** WWW allows users to create and display web pages that contains various graphics, audio, video, animation and text.

    (c) **Interactive** WWW provides interactivity using hyperlinks and input boxes (i.e. textboxes and checkboxes).

30. Read the following paragraph. Find six network and communication related abbreviations and give their expanded form alongwith a single-line definition of each of them.

The RBI is planning to expand its connectivity with all major banks of India. The plan includes providing TCP connectivity through HTTP for easy access points and seeks help from some ISPs to join hands in this venture.

Also, there is a plan to set-up IIS and SMTP servers. Some banks will go for ADSL line while others will use leased line connectivity to access these services.

The RBI is also taking help of IIT professors in this venture.   **[CBSE 2011]**

Ans. Six network and communication related abbreviations are as follows

(i) **TCP (Transmission Control Protocol)** A protocol developed for the Internet to get information from one network device to another.

(ii) **HTTP (HyperText Transfer Protocol)** A protocol that transmits hypertext over networks. This is the protocol of the web.

(iii) **ISP (Internet Service Provider)** An organisation that provides access to the Internet through various connectivity methods.

(iv) **IIS (Internet Information Server)** It is a Microsoft proprietary web server software.

(v) **SMTP (Simple Mail Transfer Protocol)** It distributes E-mail messages and attached files to one or more electronic mail boxes.

(vi) **ADSL (Asymmetrical Digital Subscriber Line)** A data communication technology that enables faster data transmission over copper telephone lines than a conventional voice band modem can provide.

Chapter Test

Multiple Choice Questions

1. .... is the part of TCP/IP that is responsible for dividing a file or message into very small parts, at the source computer.
   (a) TCP
   (b) IP
   (c) Both (a) and (b)
   (d) None of these

2. To joint the Internet, the computer has to be connected to a
   (a) Internet architecture board
   (b) Internet society
   (c) Internet service provider
   (d) None of these

3. .... is an example of text-based browser, which provides access to the Internet in the text-only mode.
   (a) Mozilla Firefox
   (b) Lynx
   (c) Internet Explorer
   (d) All of these

4. In URL, http://www.arihant.com/index.htm, which component identifies the website?
   (a) http
   (b) www.arihant.com
   (c) /index.htm
   (d) All of these

5. A domain name ending with .org belongs to
   (a) an educational institution
   (b) an organisation
   (c) a site that is highly organised
   (d) a commercial website

Short Answer Type Questions

6. Saurabh creates a website to advertise his business. He chooses an ISP to host his website.
   (i) State what Saurabh should have on home page to help users navigate his website?
   (ii) State what ISP means?

7. What is dial-up connection? Explain.

8. Below are given names of some websites
   (i) www.google.co.in
   (ii) www.microsoft.com
   Identify the components of all the web addresses given above.

9. Give any four versions of DSL technique.

10. Distinguish between web client and web server.

11. Write the advantages of blogs.

Long Answer Type Questions

12. Explain the use of the Internet in our daily lives, in education and for shopping.

13. How can you define the domain name? Also, explain domain name system.

14. Discuss about the protcols.

Answers

Multiple Choice Questions

1. (a)   2. (c)   3. (b)   4. (b)   5. (b)

For Detailed Solutions

Scan the code

CHAPTER 02

Internet Services and Mobile Technologies

In this Chapter...

- Information Retrieval
- Search Engine
- Downloading and Uploading Files from/to Remote Sites
- Web Services
- Mobile Technologies

The diversity of the services available on the Internet, makes it very popular. Out of these services, web services have expanded to become more popular. A web service is a method of communication between two electronic devices over a network.

With its help, you can retrieve or search the desired information, E-mail your friends, do video conferencing, store or retrieve files, participate in a discussion forum etc.

Information Retrieval

It is the process of accessing information that is stored on the Internet. The process of exploring and retrieving the information from the Internet is known as **net surfing**.

When your PC is connected to the Internet, you are ready to retrieve information from it. You need a particular software called **web browser** to retrieve information.

Some useful sites to visit are as follows

- **http://www.netscape.com** It contains useful information including the latest versions of web browser Netscape Navigator, list of Internet directories etc.

- **http://www.funbrain.com** It contains many educational games, math problems etc., for children. It also provides helpful stuff for teachers and parents.

- **http://www.britannica.com** It refers to the world famous encyclopedia that is now available online.

- **http://www.enwikipedia.com** It refers to free encyclopedia using wiki software.

- **http://www.crayola.com** It contains creativity tips for students, parents and educators.

Connecting your PC to Internet

To set-up an Internet connection, do the following steps

Step 1 Connect the necessary hardware like modem, ethernet cable etc, and run necessary softwares such as LAN driver.

Step 2 Make a preliminary connection using ethernet cable or a wireless connection.

Step 3 Go to the router's default IP address. e.g. 192.168.0.1.

Step 4 Set-up the Internet connection using login name **and password, which is provided by the ISP.**

Step 5 Save your settings.

Search Engine

It is a website that provides the required data on specific topics. It turns the web into a powerful tool for finding information on any topic.

Search engine allows users to enter keywords (queries or terms) related to particular topics and retrieve information about the websites containing these keywords.

When search query is submitted in the search engine by user, the software used for search algorithm scans the index to find web pages over the Internet.

Working of a Search Engine

Search engine works with three elements, which are as follows

- **Web Crawler** It is a software that browses the Internet in a systematic manner. It retrieves the information, which follows every link on the site that are stored by web search engines. It is also known as **spider**, **ant**, **automatic indexer** or **web scutter**.
- **Indexing Software** It is a software that receives the list of web documents and addresses collected by web crawler. Some search engines provide proximity search which allows users to define the distance keywords.
- **Search Algorithm** It is a concept based searching, where the research involves using statistical analysis on pages containing the words or phrases you are searching for.

Locating Sites using Search Engines

A search engine is also information retrieval system designed to find information stored on the WWW.

For searching any particular information, following steps are to be taken

Step **1** Go to the **home page** of the search engine.

Step **2** On the home page, a textbox will appear somewhere.

Step **3** In that textbox, type a **keyword** that you want to search.

Step **4** After that, there will be a button that looks like an image and has the word (such as Google Search, Web Search etc.) search written on it. Clicking on that button, search will start and will bring up a new web page with a list of websites related to that topic.

Step **5** Clicking on one of the links in the list will access that website.

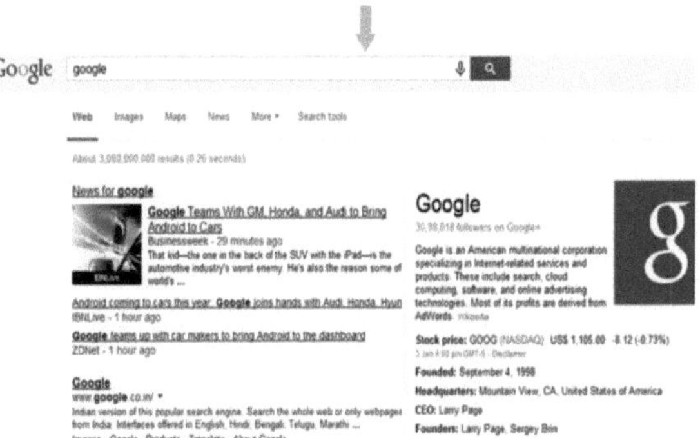

Google search web page

Many search engines also have directories or lists of topics that are organised into categories. A list of websites that contains the information are known as **hits**. The words typed in search box are called **keywords**.

The following table provides a number of operators for doing advanced searches on most search engines

Operator	What it does	Example
" "	Indicates a series of words that must appear next to each other.	"Good day sunshine" returns pages with this exact phrase.
+	Indicates that all the words must appear in the web page.	Computer + architecture will return pages that include both words computer and architecture.
−	Searches for pages that include first term but not the second.	Computer − architecture will return pages with word computer but not with an architecture.
*	Use the wildcard (*) to search for plurals or variations of words.	sing * will return pages that include a string starting with sing such as singing, sings etc.
AND, OR and NOT	Can be used in some search engines to specify your search.	Sports AND hockey, baseball OR basketball and NOT Sports.

Downloading and Uploading Files from/to Remote Sites

Downloading is the transmission of a file from server or remote computer system to user's computer. From the Internet-user's point-of-view, downloading a file means request for a file from server computer and to receive it.

The only thing is that, users must know how to find the downloaded files in the computer. If the downloaded file is an application, it must be installed, which can be an automatic operation or require the user to take one more step for running the installed program.

Uploading is the transmission of a file from local system to a server or remote computer. From an Internet-user's point-of-view, uploading is sending a file to a computer that is set-up to receive it. The most common type of uploading is when a user uploads a digital image to an Internet site.

The uploaded files are stored on the website's servers and can be seen by anyone who has the Internet connection and it is necessary to use the right software for viewing it.

Web Services

Web service is a standardized medium to propagate communication between the client and server applications on the world wide web.

Some of web services are as follows

Chat

It is the online textual or multimedia conversation. It is a real-time communication between two users *via* computer. It is widely interactive text-based communication process that takes place over the Internet.

Chatting is a virtual means of communication that involves the sending and receiving of messages, share audios and videos between users located in any part of the world.

Some popular chat applications are as follows

- WhatsApp
- WeChat
- Hike
- Facebook Messenger
- Tango

There are two basic modes for chatting on the Internet as follows

- **Text-based chat** enables communication through sending and receiving text messages.
- **Multimedia chat** enables communication through audio and video transmission.

A chat room is the hub of Internet chatting. Chat rooms (virtual rooms) are actually chat servers that allow several users to login to them simultaneously. After joining a room, you can read the messages of other users and send your own messages to them or to anyone else.

Advantages of Chat

The advantages of chat are as follows

(i) Photos can be sent using an instant messaging.

(ii) Emotions can be expressed easily when communicating with a person.

(iii) It is almost same as talking to someone face-to-face.

(iv) You can also chat in a group.

(v) It makes it possible for user to keep in contact and chat to each other even if, they are in different countries.

Disadvantages of Chat

The disadvantages of chat are as follows

(i) Viruses can be easily spread *via* texting.

(ii) Children tend to spend more time in chatting with friends instead of bonding with their family and studies.

E-mail (Electronic Mail)

It is an electronic version of sending and receiving letters. The E-mail is transmitted between computer systems, which exchange messages or pass them onto other sites according to certain Internet protocols or rules for exchanging E-mail.

For sending and receiving an E-mail, you must have an E-mail account, which is either a web based online E-mail account or an E-mail account on your ISP server.

Web based online E-mail account can be created through many sites like Gmail, Yahoo mail, Rediffmail etc.

Elements of E-mail Account

Some important elements or folders that are used to organise your E-mail messages are as follows

Inbox	It contains all incoming messages.
Outbox	The message is stored in the outbox until, it is successfully sent to the recipient.
Sent mail	It contains all sent messages.
Draft	It contains the messages, which are ready to be sent.
Trash	It contains deleted messages.
Spam	It contains junk E-mails.

Formats of an E-mail Message

There are two formats of an E-mail message, which are as follows

- **Plain text** (txt) **E-mail** It can be read by anyone type of E-mail application. It does not support text formatting options such as bold, italic, colored fonts etc. It can have attached pictures or graphics, but they cannot be inserted.
- **Rich text** (rtf) **E-mail** It cannot be read by any type of E-mail application. It supports text formatting options such as bold, italic, colored fonts etc. Pictures or graphics can also be inserted.

Structure of an E-mail Message

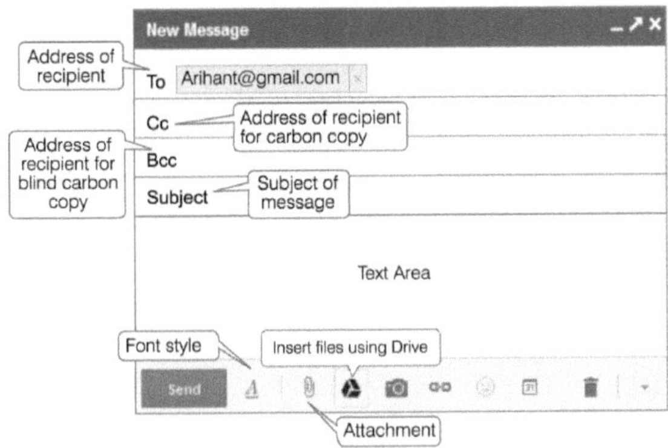

Structure of an E-mail

The general structure of an E-mail message has the following components

Components	Description
To	This field contains the E-mail address of recipient.
Cc	Cc stands for Carbon copy. This field contains the address of recipients to whom you want to send a copy of an E-mail message.
Bcc	Bcc stands for Blind carbon copy. This field also contains the list of recipients. Bcc recipients can see the To and Cc addresses but Bcc recipients name is not visible to others.
Subject	This field contains the title of a message.
Body	It includes text of an E-mail message.
Attachments	You can attach any document with E-mail message.
Formatting	Using the formatting tab, you can format the message.
Other options	Other options like emoticons, bold, italic, hyperlinks etc, are used to make messages more interactive.
Send button	You have to click the Send button to send the mail.

Emoticons

Emoticons or smileys are elements that help you to express your emotions or feelings in your E-mails and text messages.

They provide a direct and funny way to express yourself in addition to the words in your messages.

Some commonly used smileys are as follows:

Emoticon symbol	Meaning	Emoticon symbol	Meaning
:)	Smile	:D	Bigsmile
:O	Surprise	:P	Razz
;)	Wink	:(	Sad
:-O	Shouting	:	Indifferent
:~(	Crying	:@	Angry
:$	Embarrassed	*-)	Confused
<:o)	Party!	8-)	Roll Eyes

Acronyms

Apart from emoticons and symbols, you can also use acronyms and abbreviations for most frequently used words.

Some of the most widely used acronyms are as follows

Acronym	Meaning
AAMOF	as a matter of fact
BBL	be back later
BRB	be right back
BTW	by the way
CU	see you
CUL	see you later
FAQ	frequently asked questions
FTF	face-to-face
FYI	for your information
L8R	later
WB	welcome back
W8	wait

Advantages of an E-mail

The advantages of an E-mail are as follows

(i) E-mail speeds up the workflow process.

(ii) E-mailing saves papers and printing costs.

(iii) Multiple copies of a message can be sent to a group of people.

(iv) Messages can be prepared in advance and save until you are ready to send them.

(v) File and images can be attached to an E-mail.

Disadvantages of an E-mail

The disadvantages of an E-mail are as follows

(i) E-mail attachments can carry viruses.

(ii) Limited size of data file can be sent.

(iii) Hasty medium to convey emotions.

(iv) No guarantee that the mail will be read until the user logs on and check E-mail.

Video Conferencing

It is a communication technology that integrates videos and audios to connect users anywhere in the world, as if they are in the same room.

Video conferencing

This term usually refers two way communication between two or more users who are in atleast two different locations, rather than one-to-one communication and it often includes multiple people at each location.

Each user or group of users who are participating in a video conference typically must have a computer, a camera, a microphone, a video screen and a sound system.

Basically, this is a system that allows you to conduct meetings or trainings in different places simultaneously.

Some popular video conferencing applications are as follows

- Skype
- Hangouts
- IMO
- Tango
- Viber

Advantages of Video Conferencing

The advantages of video conferencing are as follows

(i) It reduces your travel costs by working remotely and also increases productivity through collaborative working.

(ii) Many people can share their videos with each other at the same time.

(iii) PowerPoint and other visual displays can be shared with everyone attending the conference at the same time.

(iv) Virtual whiteboard allows people from different locations to add their own thoughts or ideas into one collaborative space.

Disadvantages of Video Conferencing

The disadvantages of video conferencing are as follows

(i) In the middle of an important meeting, you may be disconnected at any time and have to wait to be reconnected.

(ii) There is no substitute for a face-to-face meeting in getting to know someone.

(iii) For a long time, video conferencing equipments have been expensive and out of the reach of smaller businesses.

(iv) Senders and receivers must be online at the same time.

E-Learning (Electronic Learning)

It refers to an electronic mode of delivering learning, training or educational programs to users.

E-learning is the mode of acquiring knowledge by means of Internet and computer based training programs. E-learning can be done anywhere and at anytime.

E-learning

Broadly, E-learning is synonymous with Computer Based Instruction (CBI), Computer Based Training (CBT), Internet Based Training (IBT), Web Based Training (WBT) and online education. E-learning applications and processes include web based learning, computer based learning, virtual classrooms and digital collaboration.

E-learning can be divided into the following categories

- **Synchronous** It means "at the same time," interaction of participants with an instructor *via* the web in a real-time.

- **Asynchronous** It means "not at the same time." It allows the participants to complete the web based training at their own place, without live interaction with an instructor.

Advantages of E-Learning

The advantages of E-learning are as follows

(i) Class work can be scheduled around office and family.

(ii) Reduces travel time and travel costs for off-campus students.

(iii) Self-paced learning modules allow students to work at their own pace.

(iv) Learning can accommodate different learning styles and facilitate learning through a variety of activities.

Disadvantages of E-Learning

The disadvantages of E-learning are as follows

(i) Without the routine structures of a traditional class, students may get lost or confused about course activities and deadlines.

(ii) Students may feel isolated from an instructor and classmates.

(iii) Instructor may not always be available when students are studying or need help.

E-Banking (Electronic Banking)

It is defined as the automated delivery of new and traditional banking products and services directly to the customers through an electronic and interactive communication channels. E-banking is also known as **Internet Banking**, **Online Banking** or **PC Banking**.

In Internet banking system, the bank has a centralised database, i.e. web enabled. All the services that the bank has permitted on the Internet are displayed in menu.

Customers can access E-banking services using an intelligent electronic devices, such as a Personal Computer (PC), Personal Digital Assistant (PDA), Automated Teller Machine (ATM) etc.

E-banking can be broadly classified into the two categories, which are as follows

(i) **Transactional** It involves performing financial transactions. Transactional activities are as follows

- Electronic fund transfer
- Bill payments
- Loan application and repayments
- Buying investment products

(ii) **Non-Transactional** It involves viewing bank statements. Non-transactional activities are as follows

- Account balance viewing
- Bank statement downloading
- Cheque book ordering
- Provision of account/bank statement

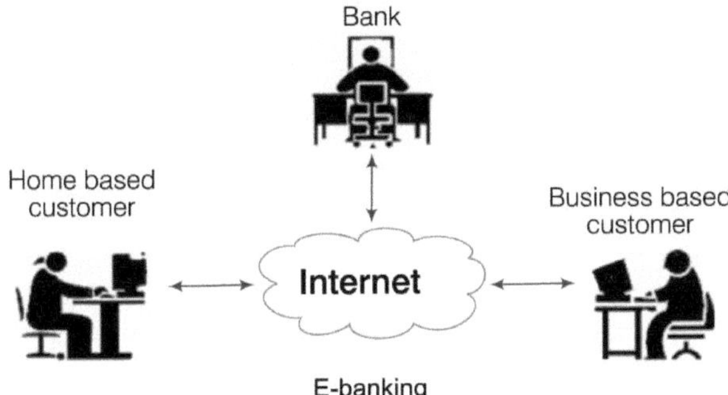

Advantages of E-Banking

The advantages of E-banking are as follows

(i) There are no geographical barriers and the services that can be offered at a minimum cost.

(ii) Through Internet banking, you can check your transactions at any time and as many times as you want to.

(iii) If the fund transfer has to be made outstation, where the bank does not have a branch, the bank would demand outstation charges, whereas with the help of online banking, it will be absolutely free for you.

(iv) Internet banking deploys the Internet as a medium for financial transaction.

Disadvantages of E-Banking

The disadvantages of E-banking are as follows

(i) Understanding the usage of Internet banking might be difficult for a beginner at the first time.

(ii) You cannot have access to Internet banking, if you do not have an Internet connection.

(iii) Security of transactions is a big issue. Your account information might get hacked by unauthorised people over the Internet.

Note *Mobile banking is a way for the customer to perform E-banking actions on his/her cell phones or other mobile devices. It is a quite popular method of banking. It might also be referred to as* ***M-banking*** *or* ***SMS banking***.

E-Shopping (Electronic Shopping)

E-shopping or Online Shopping is the process of buying goods and services from merchants who sell their products on Internet. Consumers buy a variety of items from online stores. In fact, people can purchase just about anything from companies that provide their products online.

Books, clothing, household appliances, toys, hardware, software and health insurance are just some of the hundreds of products, consumers can buy from an online store.

Some E-shopping sites are Naaptol, Flipkart, HomeShop18, Amazon.com (Prefer for buy books) etc.

Advantages of E-Shopping

The advantages of E-shopping are as follows

(i) Finding a product online is much more easier than looking for it in the local store.

(ii) Now-a-days online shopping is very reliable.

(iii) Most of the stores provide money back guarantee.

(iv) You have infinite options to choose a product.

(v) If you do not find any product within your country, then you can shop online from an international store.

Disadvantages of E-Shopping

The disadvantages of E-shopping are as follows

(i) The customer might be worried as to the similarity of the product being ordered and the product being received.

(ii) You have to wait for delivery.

(iii) You may be a victim of online fraud.

(iv) You may have to pay for shipping, while returning.

(v) You cannot really see/feel the items, you purchase.

E-Reservation (Electronic Reservation)

It means making a reservation for a service *via* Internet. You need not personally go to an office or a counter to book/reserve railways, airways tickets, hotel rooms, tourist packages etc.

Examples of E-reservation sites are as follows

- www.irctc.com
- www.makemytrip.com
- www.yatra.com
- www.bookingsite.com

Advantages of E-Reservation

The advantages of E-reservation are as follows

(i) Can access more information and find other details online about your reservation.

(ii) Websites can compare different flight prices and details.

Disadvantages of E-Reservation

The disadvantages of E-reservation are as follows
  (i) Need an Internet and PC experience.
  (ii) Might need a credit card or some other form of payment.
  (iii) If the website is not working properly, then due to some server issue, reservation cannot be done.

E-Governance (Electronic Governance)

It is the integration of Information and Communication Technology (ICT) in all the processes, with the aim of enhancing government ability to address the needs of the general public.

The basic purpose of E-governance is to simplify processes for all, i.e. government, citizens, business etc at National, State and local levels.

Types of interactions in E-governance are as follows
  - G2G (Government-to-Government)
  - G2C (Government-to-Citizen)
  - G2B (Government-to-Business)
  - G2E (Government-to-Employees)

Advantages of E-Governance

The advantages of E-governance are as follows
  (i) Cost effective
  (ii) Speed, efficiency and convenient
  (iii) Minimum use of hard copy
  (iv) Increase interest of citizens
  (v) Easily accessible

Disadvantages of E-Governance

The disadvantages of E-governance are as follows
  (i) Poor IT literacy.
  (ii) Lack of electricity in rural areas.
  (iii) Privacy problems.
  (iv) Lack of communication between different departments.

E-Groups (Electronic Groups)

An E-group or online clubbing is a group of persons or individuals who come together over the Internet for a specific or common purpose using the best Internet communication tools to share ideas, different opinions, experiences and to learn from each other.

E-groups are Internet based discussion groups. A message posted in discussion is known as **post**. All the posts are visible to all the group members.

Advantages of E-Groups

The advantages of E-groups are as follows
  (i) It helps to create and maintain social relationship.
  (ii) It facilitates communication among members.
  (iii) It facilitates research as members assist one another.
  (iv) It facilitates learning.
  (v) Less time and cost is used.
  (vi) It keeps members abreast with new development and knowledge.

Disadvantages of E-Groups

The disadvantages of E-groups are as follows
  (i) There is no privacy, if intimate issues are discussed.
  (ii) Every wrong information has a negative impact on each other.
  (iii) It is hard to follow the logical sequence of discussion.

Social Networking

It is the grouping of individuals into specific groups, like small rural communities or a neighbourhood sub-division. This service is an online service, platform or site that focuses on facilitating the building of social networks or social relations among people e.g. who share interests, activities, backgrounds or real life connections.

When it comes to online networking, social networking websites are commonly used. These websites are known as social networking sites.

Some of the different sites with their description of locating someone online are as follows

Name of Social Networking Sites	Website with their Description
Facebook	`http://www.facebook.com/` Today, Facebook is one of the largest online social networks with over 500 million people.
WhitePages	`http://www.whitepages.com/` It is used for finding basic information about people in the United States.
SuperPages	`http://www.superpages.com/` SuperPages is a online directory to find the information about people.
MySpace	`http://www.myspace.com/` MySpace is a social networking service, where people come to discover, share and connect with videos, music, images etc.
BlackPlanet	`http://www.blackplanet.com/` It is the world's largest free African, American online community where Black women and Black men meet to chat and discuss the matters.

Advantages of Social Networking

The advantages of social networking are as follows
  (i) Social networking sites help us to find our long-lost and childhood friends and relatives.
  (ii) No software or setting changes necessary to PC/phone.
  (iii) It is an easy and cost effective way to reach your consumers and people in your network.
  (iv) For business purposes, connecting with your customers on a personal and professional level will make them loyal to your company and brand.
  (v) It helps in building credibility amongst the customers.

Disadvantages of Social Networking

The disadvantages of social networking are as follows
  (i) Lack of anonymity.
  (ii) Social networking usually requires you to input your name, location, age, gender and many other types of personal information.
  (iii) Scams and harassment.
  (iv) Being online you are at risk of facing cases of cyber stalking and theft identity.
  (v) Time consuming.
  (vi) If you are new to social networking, learning process can be time consuming.

Note *Internet service was launched in India on 15 August, 1995 by Videsh Sanchar Limited.*

Mobile Technologies

Mobile technologies is a form of technology that is mostly used in cellular communication and other related aspects.

It uses a form of platform where by many transmitters have the ability to send data at the same time on a single channel. This platform is called Code Division Multiple Access (CDMA).

The mobile technology has improved from a simple device used for phone call and messaging into a multitasking device used for GPS navigation, Internet browsing, gaming, instant messaging tool, etc.

Some terms related to mobile technologies are as follows

3G (Third Generation)

3G is short for Third Generation of mobile telecommunications technology also called Tri-Band 3G.

3G telecommunication networks support services that provide the information transfer rate of atleast 200 Kbps.

It adds multimedia facilities that allow video, audio and graphics applications. However, many services advertised as 3G provides higher speed than the minimum technical requirements for a 3G service.

4G (Fourth Generation)

In telecommunications, 4G is the Fourth Generation of mobile phone communication standards. It is a successor of the Third Generation (3G) standard.

A 4G system provides mobile ultra-broadband Internet access. It is based on packet switching only and these systems are projected to provide speeds up to 100 Mbps while moving and 1 Gbps while stationary.

Two 4G candidate systems are commercially deployed the mobile WiMAX standard (at first in South Korea in 2006) and the first release Long Term Evolution (LTE) standard (in Oslo, Norway since 2009).

SMS (Short Message Service)

SMS, commonly referred to as text messaging, is a service for sending short messages of up to 160 characters to mobile devices, including cellular phones, smartphones and PDAs.

SMS are transmitted within the same cell or to anyone with roaming service capability.

MMS (Multimedia Messaging Service)

MMS is mobile phone service that allows users to send multimedia messages to each other. This includes images, videos and sound files. MMS is an extension of SMS, which is used to send and receive text messages.

MMS support is typically integrated into the text messaging interface and activates automatically when needed.

Chapter Practice

Objective Questions

• Multiple Choice Questions

1. A search engine is a program to search
  (a) for information
  (b) web pages
  (c) web pages for specified index terms
  (d) web pages for information using specified search terms

Ans. (*d*) A search engine is a program to search web pages for information using specified search items.

2. Which of the following statements about search engine is true? **[CBSE 2011]**
  (a) Search engines discriminate between good and bad sites.
  (b) Search engines have fixed hours, when we can use them.
  (c) Search engines are waste of time as they do not provide relevant information.
  (d) Search engine is a program designed to search for information on the web using keywords.

Ans. (*d*) Search engine is a program designed to search for information on the web using keywords. It turns the web into a powerful tool for finding information on any topic.

3. A software that searches through a database of web pages for particular information is known as
  (a) domain
  (b) E-mail client
  (c) modem
  (d) search engine

Ans. (*d*) Search engine is a software that searches through a database of web pages for particular information.

4. Which software browses the Internet in a systematic manner? **[CBSE 2013]**
  (a) Web crawler
  (b) Web browser
  (c) Indexing software
  (d) Search algorithm

Ans. (*a*) Web crawler software browses the Internet in a systematic manner. Web search engine works by storing information about many web pages, retrieved by a web crawler.

5. Shri wants to search about computer vendor in Meerut excluding Dell category. Which of the following search query best suits his requirements?
  (a) Computer vendor Meerut Dell
  (b) Computer vendor Meerut not Dell
  (c) Computer vendor + Meerut – Dell
  (d) Computer vendor + Meerut + Dell

Ans. (*c*) Shri wants to search about computer vendor in Meerut excluding Dell category. The best search query used by him is Computer vendor + Meerut – Dell.

6. When we copy a web page or a file from a server to our local computer, this process is called
  (a) conferencing
  (b) downloading
  (c) uploading
  (d) None of these

Ans. (*b*) When we copy a web page or a file from a server to our local computer, this process is called downloading. Downloading a file means request for a file from server computer and to receive it.

7. Image files uploaded and downloaded over the Internet can be processed with a compression application. Why are image files compressed before transmitted over Internet?
  (a) To increase security
  (b) To make them easier to open
  (c) To reduce transmission time
  (d) To improve the quality of images.

Ans. (*c*) Image files are compressed before transmitted over Internet to reduce transmission time.

8. Identify the software that helps you in sending and receiving an E-mail.
  (a) MS-Office
  (b) Internet Explorer
  (c) Gmail
  (d) None of these

Ans. (*c*) Gmail is preferred E-mail client which is used for sending or receiving an E-mail. It is free E-mail service introduced by Google.

9. Bcc field contains the list of recipients. Bcc stands for **[CBSE 2014]**
  (a) Basic carbon copy
  (b) Blind carbon copy
  (c) Blind client copy
  (d) Basic client copy

Ans. (*b*) Bcc denotes the Blind carbon copy. It contains the list of recipients. It can see the To and Cc addresses.

10. A two way video conversation among multiple participants is called
(a) video chatting   (b) video talking
(c) video conferencing   (d) video watching

Ans. (*c*) A two way video conversation among multiple participants is called video conferencing. Two or more people hear and see each other, share white board and other applications through video conferencing.

11. .... services typically include reviewing account activity and balance, sending electronic payments and transferring funds between accounts electronically.
(a) E-banking   (b) E-reservation
(c) E-posting   (d) E-mail

Ans. (*a*) E-banking provides all transactional and non-transactional activities electronically. E-banking services include reviewing account activity and balance, sending electronic payments and transferring funds between accounts electronically.

12. Which of the following sites, would you prefer to buy books?   **[CBSE 2011]**
(a) www.yahoomail.com   (b) www.sun.com
(c) www.msn.com   (d) www.amazon.com

Ans. (*d*) www.amazon.com is the world's largest online retailer and a best site for buying books.

13. E-reservation is a process of making reservations of
(a) tickets   (b) hotel rooms
(c) tourists packages   (d) All of these

Ans. (*d*) E-reservation is a process of making reservation of tickets, hotel rooms, tourists packages etc. You can access more information and find other details online about your reservation.

14. Which mobile technology system provides mobile ultra-broadband Internet access?
(a) 3G   (b) 4G
(c) SMS   (d) MMS

Ans. (*b*) 4G stands for Fourth Generation. It provides mobile ultra-broadband Internet access. It is based on packet switching only.

• Case Based MCQs

Direction *Read the case and answer the following questions.*

15. It is a website that provides the required data on specific topics. It turns the web into a powerful tool for finding information on any topic. Search engine allows users to enter keywords (queries or terms) related to particular topics and retrieve information about the websites containing these keywords. It is a program designed to search for information on the web through a database of web page's queries or keywords.

When search query is submitted in the search engine by user, the software used for search algorithm scans the index to find web pages over the Internet.

(i) Which of the following is an example of search engine?
(a) Google   (b) AltaVista
(c) Yahoo   (d) All of these

(ii) The words typed in search box are called
(a) keywords   (b) hit words
(c) search words   (d) All of these

(iii) A list of websites that contains the information are known as ....
(a) miss   (b) success   (c) hits   (d) yahoo

(iv) Which search engine is also known as spider, web scutter, etc?
(a) Google   (b) Web crawler
(c) Yahoo   (d) Hotbot

(v) Search engine is also a/an
(a) information retrieval   (b) information storage
(c) process information   (d) None of these

Ans. (i) (*d*) Search engine is a website that provides the required data on specific topics. Google, AltaVista, Yahoo, Hotbot, Bing etc., are examples of search engine.

(ii) (*a*) The words typed in search box are called keywords. Search engines search these keywords and provide information related to this keyword.

(iii) (*c*) Many search engines also have directories or lists of topics that are organised into categories. A list of websites that contains the information are known as hits.

(iv) (*b*) Web crawler search engine is also known as spider, web scutter etc. It browses the Internet in a systematic manner.

(v) (*a*) A search engine is also an information retrieval system designed to find information stored on the WWW.

16. It is an electronic version of sending and receiving letters. The E-mail is transmitted between computer systems, which exchange messages or pass them onto other sites according to certain Internet protocols or rules for exchanging E-mail. You can send E-mail from your computer at anytime to any address around the world and your electronic letter or E-mail will arrive at its destination in seconds after you send it, even if the receiver is not online.

For sending and receiving an E-mail, you must have an E-mail account, which is either a web based online E-mail account or an E-mail account on your ISP server. Web based online E-mail account can be created through many sites like Gmail, Yahoo mail, Rediffmail etc.

(i) Which among the following is an area of E-mail that is short description of the message?

   (a) Subject   (b) Cc

   (c) Bcc   (d) Attachment

(ii) Which of the following is always a part of E-mail address?

   (a) Period(.)   (b) At sign(@)

   (c) Space( )   (d) Underscore(_)

(iii) An E-mail attachment is referred to as

   (a) the body of the E-mail

   (b) the address of the sender

   (c) a document that is sent with an E-mail

   (d) any document that can be attached and sent with an E-mail

(iv) Which of the following is not an E-mail service provider?

   (a) Hotmail (b) Gmail   (c) Bing   (d) Yahoo mail

(v) Sending an E-mail is similar to

   (a) writing a letter   (b) drawing a picture

   (c) talking on the phone   (d) sending a package

Ans. (i) (*a*) Subject is the component of E-mail message that shows the short description of the message. It displays in most E-mail systems that list E-mail message individually.

   (ii) (*b*) At sign @ is always a part of E-mail address. It is used as an separator. An E-mail address is generally of the form username@domain_name.

   (iii) (*d*) An E-mail attachment is referred to as any document that can be attached and sent with an E-mail. Some E-mails could be attached with files such as text, image, etc.

   (iv) (*c*) Bing is not an E-mail service provider. It is a search engine.

   (v) (*a*) Sending an E-mail is similar to writing a letter.

PART 2

Subjective Questions

• Short Answer Type Questions

1. What is search engine? What is its usage? Give example.

or What is a search engine? Give one example of search engine.   **[CBSE 2006, 02]**

Ans. A search engine is a website that lets you search the Internet for websites on specific topics. Search engines turn the web into a powerful tool for finding information on any topic. There are several benefits of using search engine like,

   (i) Search engines do have the ability to provide refined or more precise results.

   (ii) Search engine provides a wealth of information for professional and personal use.
   e.g. Google.

2. When using a search engine, what does a minus sign used with keywords in the search box mean?

Ans. Search engine is a website that provides the required data on specific content. It also allows users to enter keywords related to particular topics and retrieve information. The minus sign in front of a word or phrase means that it includes first term but not the second term.

3. Why uploading and downloading a file is required? Explain with example.

or What is the need of uploading and downloading files?

Ans. When we need a file which is located at the server end, we have to download the file that means transmission of file from server to user's computer. Similarly, if we want to share something like file, picture etc., we have to upload that file or picture on the Internet that means transmission of file from user computer to server.

4. What is chatting? Is it necessary to be online while chatting?

Ans. Chatting is the textual or multimedia conversation over the Internet. It is a real-time communication between two users *via* computer. It is widely interactive text based communication process that takes place over the Internet. Yes, it is necessary to be online, while chatting.

5. What is an E-mail? Write two advantages of an E-mail.   **[CBSE 2012, 10]**

Ans. E-mail (Electronic mail) is a popular Internet service, which is used for sending or receiving messages electronically over a computer network.

The advantages of an E-mail are as follows

   (i) E-mail is a cost effective medium of communication.

   (ii) Ease of use.

6. Mention some disadvantages of an E-mail.

Ans. Some disadvantages of an E-mail are as follows

   (i) E-mail attachment can carry viruses.

   (ii) Limited size of data file can be sent.

   (iii) Hasty medium to convey emotions.

   (iv) Non guarantee that the mail will be read until the user logs on and check E-mail.

7. Briefly explain the significance of video conferencing. **[CBSE 2019]**

Ans. (i) Video conferencing reduces your travel costs by working remotely and also increases productivity through collaborative working.

(ii) Many people can share their videos with each other at the same time.

8. What is E-learning? Explain any two merits of E-learning. **[Specimen Paper 2020]**

Ans. E-learning refers to an electronic mode of delivering learning, training or educational programs to users. It is the mode of acquiring knowledge by means of Internet and computer based training programs. E-learning can be done anywhere and at anytime.

Two merits of E-learning are as follows :

(i) Reduces travel time and travel costs for off-campus students.

(ii) Develops knowledge of an Internet and computer skills that will help learners throughout their lives and careers.

9. Write the full form of Cc and Bcc (used in E-mail communication). Explain the difference between them. **[Specimen Paper 2020]**

Ans. Cc stands for Carbon copy and Bcc stands for Blind carbon copy.

In Cc, all recipients will be able to see each other mail address. Whereas, in Bcc none of the recipient will be able to see each other mail address.

10. Mention the services which are provided by transactional category of E-banking. **[CBSE 2014]**

Ans. Transactional category of E-banking involves performing financial transaction. Transactional activities are as follows

(i) Electronic fund transfer

(ii) Bill payments

(iii) Loan application and repayments

(iv) Buying investment products

11. What do you mean by E-shopping? Give three advantages of it. **[CBSE 2015]**

Ans. E-shopping or Online Shopping is the process of buying goods and services from merchants who sell their products on Internet. Consumers buy a variety of items from online stores. In fact, people can purchase just about anything from companies that provide their products online.

The advantages of E-shopping are as follows

(i) Finding a product online is much more easier than looking for it in the local store.

(ii) Now-a-days online shopping is very reliable.

(iii) Most of the stores provide money back guarantee.

12. What are the differences between MMS and SMS?

Ans. Differences between MMS and SMS are as follows

MMS	SMS
MMS stands for Multimedia Messaging Service.	SMS stands for Short Message Service.
MMS are used to send multimedia files attaching with a message such as pictures, music, audio and video.	SMS is used for sending text based messages including symbols and emoji.

13. What are E-groups? **[CBSE 2018]**

Ans. An E-groups is a group of persons who come together over the Internet for a specific or common purpose using the best Internet communication tools to share ideas, different opinions, experiences and to learn from each other.

14. Rani is researching history of computers on the Internet. She uses a search engine.

(i) The computer sometimes takes a long time to respond when Rani enters a question into the search engine. Give a reason why this might happen?

(ii) The search engine returned a large number of links when she entered computers. What should Rani do to reduce the number of links?

Ans. (i) Due to slow Internet connection.

(ii) She should write 'history of computers'.

15. Describe the following social networking sites:

(i) Facebook   (ii) MySpace

Ans. (i) **Facebook** It was developed by Mark Zuckerberg. Today, facebook is one of the largest online social networks with over 500 million users. It is the one site where you are likely to find friends, colleagues and relatives all floating around.

(ii) **MySpace** It is a social networking website offering an interactive, user submitted network of friends, personal profiles, blogs, photos, music and videos. It was the largest social networking site in the world.

• Long Answer Type Questions

16. When using a search engine to search, then would you use quotation marks around search terms? **[CBSE 2007]**

Ans. Quotation marks should be used around a phrase or search terms. Surrounding terms with quotation marks limit the search results to only those web pages that contain the exact phrase, we have specified.

Doing this ensures that, the concept will be searched for as a whole and not picked apart by the search engine or we can say, without the quotation marks, the results will include any page that contains the words we have used regardless of what order those words are in.

17. Transferring files through E-mail is restricted due to file size. Justify.

Ans. Over the Internet, a message will often pass through several mail transfer agents to reach the recipients. Each of these has to store the message before forwarding it on and many therefore, need to impose size limits.

The result is that while large attachments may internally send within an organisation, they are unreliable when sending across Internet.

e.g. In general, 10 MB is considered safe for the maximum size of an E-mail but, Google's gmail service increased its limit to 25 MB.

18. List some advantages and disadvantages of an E-mail.

Ans. The advantages of an E-mail are as follows

(i) **Low cost** We can send the E-mail to other person at a very low cost. It requires only Internet connection cost to send the E-mail.

(ii) **Speed** E-mail can be sent at a very high speed.

(iii) **Waste reduction** E-mail goes a long way towards reducing the cluster of papers in the modern office, not to mention saving many trees.

(iv) **Ease of use** It is easy to send an E-mail as compared to traditional letter.

The disadvantages of an E-mail are as follows

(i) **Hardware requirement** You need a computer to read or print E-mail.

(ii) **Impermanent** Your sent mail messages can be altered in all the ways.

(iii) **A hasty medium** It is a limitation because E-mail is so easy to use, it is also easy to send a message that you later regret.

(iv) **Hard to convey emotions** Without the extra clues of voice, posture and expression, it is difficult to understand what someone really means in a message.

19. Write short notes on the following terms

(i) Information retrieval   (ii) E-banking

(iii) Online shopping   (iv) E-reservation

(v) E-groups   **[CBSE 2014]**

Ans. (i) **Information retrieval** It refers to the process of accessing the information that is stored on the Internet.

(ii) **E-banking** It refers to the automated delivery of new and traditional banking products and services directly to customers over the Internet.

(iii) **Online shopping** It refers to the activity of purchasing items from different websites on Internet.

(iv) **E-reservation** It refers to the process that helps users to reserve movie, train and airline tickets as well as hotel rooms through Internet.

(v) **E-groups** It refers to an online environment where users sharing common views and ideas that come together to meet and discuss topics of their interest.

20. What are the dangers associated with social networking?   **[CBSE 2013]**

Ans. Dangers associated with social networking are as follows

(i) **Lack of anonymity** Social networking usually requires you to input your name, location, age, gender and many other types of personal information.

(ii) **Scams and harassment** Being online you are at risk of facing cases of harassment, cyber stalking, online scams and theft identity.

(iii) **Time consuming** If you are new on social networking, learning the process can be very time consuming.

(iv) **The illusion of security** The Internet is definitely not secured as social or human hackers can hack one's personal account.

(v) **Isolation** Social networking sites do not provide isolation. As, once information is posted on a social networking site, it is no longer private.

21. Somya wants to collect some information regarding the history of India.

(i) What is the fastest and easiest way of doing this, which saves her efforts as well?

(ii) Write down the following steps in the correct order to show, how Somya could find information.

(a) Type keywords.

(b) Look at the list of websites starting at the top.

(c) Load a search engine.

(d) Click the search button.

(e) Open the web browser.

Ans. (i) Online search using search engine.

(ii) (e) Open the web browser

(c) Load a search engine

(a) Type keywords

(d) Click the search button

(b) Look at the list of websites starting at the top.

22. Sharvan Joshi is a student of Political Science and is a keen researcher of political issues related to various countries and states. He wants to share his research and his own opinions on these issues on day-to-day basis with everyone on World Wide Web (WWW).

He is also interested in collecting views of others to enhance his research and knowledge related to his area of interest. He belongs to a middle class family and cannot afford his own Website. Also being a non-technical person he cannot create a dynamic Website to deal with day-to-day inputs.

(i) Suggest an easy way for Sharvan to achieve the same.

(ii) Also, name two popularly used free services that can help Sharvan in this regard.

(iii) Sharvan wants to search some information on political issues, which program or service will help him? Also, explain this service.

Ans. (i) Sharvan should develop a blog.

(ii) Twitter and Facebook.

(iii) Search engine will him to search information. It is a website that provides the required data on specific topics. It turns the web into a powerful tool for finding information on any topic. Search engine allows users to enter keywords (queries or terms) related to particular topics and retrieve information about the websites containing these keywords. It is a program designed to search for information on the web through a database of web page's queries or keywords.

23. Gargi set-up the following Auto Delete options on her Web-based E-mail account.

Inbox	Never
Sent	Never
Draft	Never
Personal	Never
User created	Never
Trash	Older than 1 month
Filtered spam	Submit

What is the most likely reason, she has set the Trash folder to delete 'Older than 1 month'?

Gargi wants

(a) all E-mails to have a delete date.

(b) sent all E-mails to be deleted after 1 month.

(c) deleted all E-mails to only remain in the Trash folder for 1 month.

(d) all E-mails in her inbox to be moved to the Trash folder after 1 month.

Ans. (c) Gargi wants deleted all E-mails to only remain in the Trash folder for 1 month.

24. As life gets busy, it becomes difficult for everyone to keep track with school and college friends, old colleagues, old neighbours and favourite teachers. It is important to keep in touch with all your near and dear ones. At times, people sitting miles away doing similar kind of activity or solving similar kind of problems can help you to achieve goals faster by sharing their experience.

Similarly, people belonging to different socio-economic background can change your perspective and can enhance your understanding of various cultures.

[CBSE 2011]

(i) Suggest any two real-time tools that are suitable for the above mentioned activities.

(ii) What is the generic name used for such tools?

Ans. (i) Twitter and Facebook.

(ii) Social networking.

Chapter Test

Multiple Choice Questions

1. How can you send E-mail to more than one recipient at the same time?
(a) By sending an E-mail with a notice to be forwarded to the rest of the recipients
(b) This is not possible at this time
(c) By adding a second recipient in the "Cc" field
(d) By adding all recipient's E-mail address in the "To" field separated by semicolon

2. Which one of following is a search engine?
(a) Google
(b) Rediffmail
(c) India times
(d) Yahoo mail

3. It is the way for the customer to perform E-banking actions on his/her cell phones.
(a) E-banking
(b) E-reservation
(c) M-banking
(d) M-reservation

4. Symbols used to express emotions in an E-mail are known as
(a) emoticons
(b) cartoons
(c) E-symbols
(d) None of these

5. Which of the following is/are example of video conferencing applications?
(a) Skype
(b) Tango
(c) Hangouts
(d) All of these

Short Answer Type Questions

6. Mawana Sugar Private Limited has a head office located in Mawana and a large number of branches nationwise. The head office used video conferencing to communicate with the branch managers.
(i) Identify the requirements to be filled by each branch for video conferencing.
(ii) Give some advantages of using video conferencing.

7. Raman is the owner of a small company that manufactures toys for children. He decided that it would be beneficial to the company to create a website, which would allow customers to order online.
(i) Give one advantage of using the Internet to purchase goods.
(ii) Explain how a customer who did not know the company's website address, could gain access to the site?

8. What are the advantages of chat?

9. Karan uses a search engine to get detail regarding India struggle for freedom.
(i) Define the word search engine.
(ii) Name any five common search engines.

10. What is emoticons? Also, write some commonly used smileys.

Long Answer Type Questions

11. Discuss the structure of an E-mail message.

12. Give the benefits of social networking.

13. Define the following terms
(i) Chat
(ii) Video Conferencing
(iii) E-shopping
(iv) E-governance
(v) Social Networking

Answers

Multiple Choice Questions

1. (c)   *2. (a)*   *3. (c)*   *4. (a)*   *5. (d)*

For Detailed Solutions
Scan the code

CHAPTER 03

Working with Tables in HTML

In this Chapter...

- Basic Table Tags in HTML
- < TABLE > Tag
- < TD > Tag
- < TR > and < TH > Tags
- Tables : Header, Body and Footer
- Event Handling in HTML Tables

Tables are great way to layout the HTML web pages. Tables allow a user to display tabular data on web pages in a very clear and uniform way. It is an orderly arrangement of data that is stored in the form of rows and columns, therefore web developers use tables very frequently in their web pages.

Basic Table Tags in HTML

In HTML, tables are created by <TABLE> tag. Data of tables can be in form of text or graphics. These tables are made up of rows and columns. An intersection of a row and a column is known as **cell**. The data in tables is contained in cells.

Basic tags that are used to create a table in HTML are as follows

(i) **Table Tags** (<TABLE>....</TABLE>) It is used to insert a table in a web page. It is a first tag, which starts and closes a table.

(ii) **Row Tags** (<TR>....</TR>) It is used to define a table rows. Table rows are group of the header, footer and body sections that is created by using thead, tfoot and tbody elements. Generally, the first row of a table is referred to as the **header section**, the last row of a table is referred to as the **footer section** and the middle rows in the table are referred to as the **body section**.

(iii) **Cell Tags** (<TD>....</TD>, <TH>....</TH>) These are used to define data cells (current cells) or header of the table. These tags are the data containers of the table. They can contain all sorts of HTML elements like : text, images, lists, other tables, etc.

(iv) **Caption Tags** (<CAPTION>....</CAPTION>) It is used to define the title or caption for the table that provides a short description of the table's purpose.

To Create a Table

Here is an example of HTML code for creating a table:

```
<HTML>
  <HEAD> <TITLE> Table </TITLE> </HEAD>
  <BODY>
    <TABLE>
      <CAPTION> Name of Students</CAPTION>
        <TR>
            <TD> Sunita </TD>
            <TD> Amita </TD>
            <TD> Ameesha </TD>
        </TR>
        <TR>
            <TD> Ankita </TD>
```

```
        <TD> Prachi </TD>
        <TD> Neha   </TD>
      </TR>
      <TR>
        <TD> Esha </TD>
        <TD> Preeti </TD>
        <TD> Payal </TD>
      </TR>
    </TABLE>
  </BODY>
</HTML>
```

Output

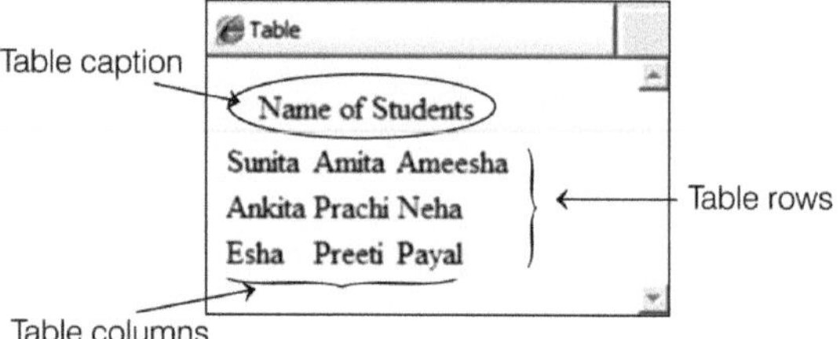

In the above code, we used a <TABLE> tag which specifies a table that is to be inserted. After <TABLE> tag, it arrives a <CAPTION> tag, this <CAPTION> tag is used to add headline in the table. Here, the caption is 'Name of Students'. After <CAPTION> tag, <TR> tag is used which specifies a new table row. There should be a </TR> tag in the end of each row.

Here, <TR> tag is mentioned three times. This means that three rows are added. The next tag is <TD>, which denotes the data cells.

It has been put in front of every piece of information that you want to add in a cell and <TD> tag is mentioned three times in each <TR> tag, i.e. each row will contain three data cells. At the end, the </TABLE> tag closes a table.

<TABLE> Tag

This tag is used to create tables in HTML. The table tags in HTML are <TABLE> and </TABLE>. Everything to be put in a table, should be enclosed between these two tags. Since, <TABLE> is a container tag thus both the tags, i.e. opening and closing are required.

Syntax

```
<TABLE>
  :
</TABLE>
```

Within the <TABLE> tags, a variety of attributes can be added to determine the look of table.

You can specify width of the table, add border, background color, spacing between cells (cellspacing) and spacing between border of the cell and its content (cellpadding) in a table.

The various attributes of <TABLE> tag discussed in detail are as follows

(i) border Attribute

A border can be added to a table by using border attribute. The border attribute of <TABLE> tag accepts values in pixels. The thickness of border can be adjusted as per the user's requirement.

By default, value of the border attribute is 0 (zero), i.e. no border is displayed in your table.

(ii) bordercolor Attribute

This attribute is used to specify the color of the table's border. Color of your choice for the border to make it more attractive or to make its appearance consistent with the other tables in your web page.

(iii) frame Attribute

This attribute specifies which part of the table's borders will be visible. Hence, the frame attribute will always be used with the border attribute. The values that can be specified for frames are as follows

- **void** outside borders are not shown.
- **above** top edge of the border is shown.
- **below** bottom edge of the border is shown.
- **hsides** top and bottom edges of the border are shown.
- **lhs** left edge of the border is shown.
- **rhs** right edge of the border is shown.
- **vsides** left and right edges of the border are shown.
- **box** all edges are shown on all four sides (like border).
- **border** all edges are shown on all four sides (default).

Thus, frame attribute contains 9 types of values that all can be specified for frames.

(iv) rules Attribute

This attribute also works with border attribute of <TABLE> tag. The rules attribute defines which lines or rules to draw between rows and columns in your table.

The basic difference between the frame attribute and rules attribute is that the frame attribute is used to display a specific outer portion of a table border while the rules attribute is used to display a specific inside portion of a table border. The values that can be specified for rules attribute are as follows

- **none** no rules are drawn or hides all interior borders.
- **groups** rules are drawn between row groups and column groups.
- **rows** rules are drawn between rows only.
- **cols** rules are drawn between columns only.
- **all** rules are drawn between all rows and all columns.

Thus, rules attribute contains 5 types of values that all can be specified for rules.

(v) cellpadding and cellspacing Attributes

cellpadding is used to specify the space (in pixels) between the borders of the cell and contents of the cell. cellspacing is used to set the distance between two cells.

To control the spacing in the cells, the cellspacing and cellpadding attributes are used.

(vi) align Attribute

This attribute allows you to change the position of the table in a web page. It can have values left, right and center. The align attribute of <TABLE> tag aligns complete table with respect to the text in the browser.

(vii) background Attribute

This attribute is used to set an image in the background of the table. It enables you to modify the background of your tables in HTML. You can specify an image by putting its path as the value of background attribute to set it as a background of the table.

(viii) bgcolor Attribute

This attribute specifies the background color of a table. With bgcolor, you need to specify the desired background color. By default, background color of the table is white.

(ix) height and width Attributes

You can set the height and width of the table using height and width attributes. Height and width are specified in terms of pixels or percentage of the browser window.

(x) summary Attribute

This attribute is used to provide extra information about the table and its contents. It is useful for non-visual web browsers. This attribute has no visual effect in ordinary web browsers.

<TD> Tag

The <TD> tag is used to specify a cell or table data within a table. Here, TD stands for Table Data. It is a container tag and that is why it must contain matching closing </TD> tag. This tag can only be present inside <TR> ... </TR> tag.

Note *Combining two or more cells in a table on a web page is called* **Spanning***.*

e.g. To show the use of <TD> tag.

```
<HTML>
  <HEAD><TITLE> TD Tag </TITLE></HEAD>
  <BODY>
    <TABLE>
        <TR> <TD> The td attribute </TD>
    </TR>
    </TABLE>
  </BODY>
</HTML>
```

Output

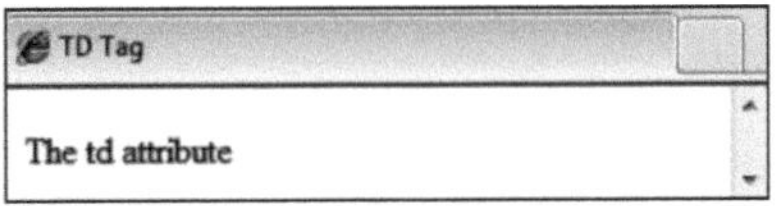

The various attributes of <TD> tag are as follows

(i) align Attribute

The table data can be aligned using align attribute. The align attribute is used with <TD> tag. It can have any one of the three values–left, right and center. By default, the content of a cell in a table is left aligned.

(ii) width Attribute

This attribute is used to define the width of the cells in the table. It is used with <TD> tag. The width of the cells is defined either in pixels or in percentage.

(iii) height Attribute

This attribute specifies the height of a cell. Normally, a cell takes up the space it needs to display the content. The height attribute is used to set a predefined height of a cell.

(iv) bgcolor Attribute

In HTML, background of a table together with colors of rows and columns can be changed.

When bgcolor is used with <TABLE> tag, it sets a background color for the entire table. On the other hand, when bgcolor is used with <TR> tag, it sets a background color for an individual row. When bgcolor is used with <TD> tag, it sets a background color for an individual table cell.

Note *Changing the color of any particular row or cell does not affect the background color of rest of the table.*

(v) background Attribute

An image can also be inserted as the background image of a single cell. When background attribute is used with <TABLE> tag, it sets a background image for the entire table. On the other hand, when background attribute is used with <TR> tag, it sets a background image for an individual row. When background attribute is used with <TD> tag, it sets a background image for an individual table cell.

(vi) rowspan and colspan Attributes

In HTML, uniform grid of columns and rows are created. But sometimes, we need some of the cells to be combined, and for this purpose, rowspan and colspan attributes are used. The colspan attribute allows the user to stretch a cell to span multiple columns (merge two or more columns). On the other hand, rowspan attribute is used to span multiple rows (merge two or more rows).

The attributes, colspan (how many across) and rowspan (how many down) indicate, how many columns or rows, a cell should take up.

Example of rowspan and colspan attributes is shown below

```
<TD rowspan = "2"> </TD>
<TD colspan = "2"> </TD>
```

Here, the rowspan attribute will merge two rows and colspan attribute will merge two columns.

(vii) valign Attribute

This attribute determines the placement of content in a cell. This attribute is used in <TD> tag to set the vertical alignment of that particular cell's content, when the cell have span of more than one rows. The values that can be used are as follows

- **Top** It will put the text as close to the top of the cell as it is possible.
- **Middle** It will center the text in the cell.
- **Bottom** It will put the text as close to the bottom of the cell as it is possible.

<TR> and <TH> Tags

The <TR> tag stands for Table Row. This tag is used to create a new row of data in a table. The <TR> tag also uses similar attributes as that of <TD> tag except rowspan and colspan. This tag can only be present inside <TABLE> tag. The <TD> tag have higher priority than <TR> tag.

The <TH> tag stands for Table Header. This tag is used for specifying a table's header. It displays the content of a table in heading style and this content appears in bold. This is the only difference between <TH> and <TD> tags. <TH> accepts the similar attributes as that of <TD> tag.

e.g. To show the use of <TR> and <TH> tags.

```
<HTML>
  <HEAD><TITLE> Table </TITLE></HEAD>
  <BODY>
    <TABLE border="1" cellpadding="15">
      <TR>
        <TH> Tag </TH> <TH> Stands For </TH>
      </TR>
      <TR>
        <TD> tr </TD> <TD> Table Row </TD>
      </TR>
      <TR>
        <TD> th </TD> <TD> Table Header </TD>
      </TR>
    </TABLE>
  </BODY>
</HTML>
```

Output

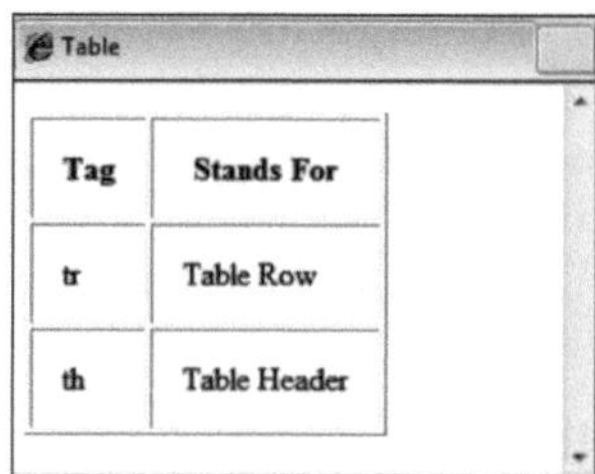

Tables: Header, Body and Footer

Tables can be divided into three portions as a head, a body and a foot. The head and foot are rather similar to headers and footers in a word processor document that remain the same for every page, while the body is the main content holder of the table.

The three elements for separating the head, body and foot of a table are as follows

(i) **<THEAD>** indicates that a group of rows are the header rows at the top of the table.

(ii) **<TBODY>** indicates that a group of rows are the body rows or main body of the table.

(iii) **<TFOOT>** indicates that a group of rows are the footer rows at the bottom of the table.

A table may contain several <TBODY> elements to indicate different pages or groups of data.

Browsers can use these elements to enable scrolling of the table body independently of the header and footer. Also, when printing a large table that spans multiple pages, these elements can enable the table header and footer to be printed at the top and bottom of each page.

The <THEAD>, <TBODY> and <TFOOT> tags contain various attributes such as align, bgcolor and valign.

e.g. To show the use of <THEAD>, <TBODY> and <TFOOT> tags.

```
<HTML>
  <HEAD> <TITLE> Table </TITLE> </HEAD>
  <BODY>
    <TABLE border="2">
      <THEAD bgcolor="grey">
        <TR>
          <TD> Student_Name </TD>
          <TD> Roll_No </TD>
          <TD> Percentage </TD>
        </TR>
      </THEAD>
      <TBODY bgcolor="pink">
        <TR>
```

```
            <TD> Amita </TD>
            <TD> 18 </TD>
            <TD> 81 </TD>
        </TR>
        <TR>
            <TD> Anupriya </TD>
            <TD> 20 </TD>
            <TD> 89 </TD>
        </TR>
    </TBODY>
    <TFOOT bgcolor="yellow">
        <TR>
            <TD> Sanjay </TD>
            <TD> 21 </TD>
            <TD> 79 </TD>
        </TR>
    </TFOOT>
    </TABLE>
  </BODY>
</HTML>
```

Output

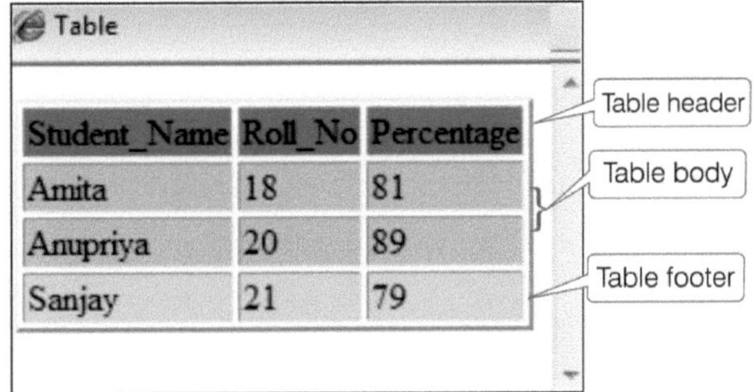

Event Handling in HTML Tables

In HTML, events are features that allow users to add interactivity between the web page and its visitor. An event is an action that is performed by the user, such as by pressing a key or on mouse click. An event handler allows you to run a particular code, which is associated with that particular event. An event is activated, when you click the object, on which you apply the event. Some of the events available for HTML are given below:

offline, onchange, onclick, ondrag, onerror, onfocus, oninput, oninvalid, ononline, onselect, onwaiting etc.

e.g. To illustrate the use of event handling.

```
<HTML>
    <HEAD> <TITLE> Table with Event Handling
    </TITLE> </HEAD>
    <BODY>
        <TABLE border="2" onclick=
        "alert('This is event handling in HTML
        tables')">
            <TR>
                <TD> One </TD> <TD> Two </TD>
            </TR>
            <TR>
                <TD> Three </TD> <TD> Four </TD>
            </TR>
        </TABLE>
    </BODY>
</HTML>
```

Output

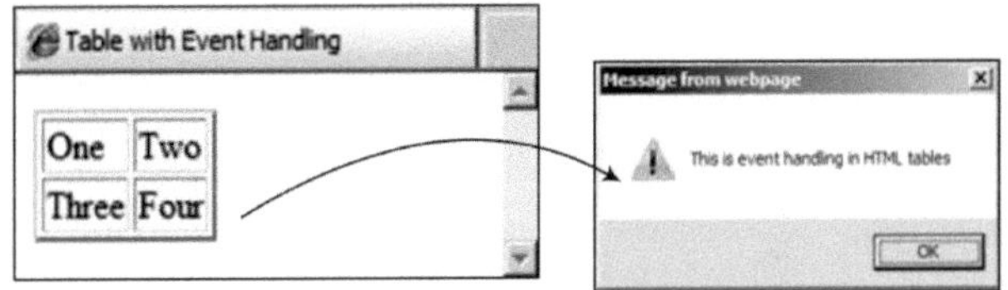

onclick event is activated when you click the object (table) on which you apply the event.

Note When you click anywhere on the table, a message box will appear. In this message box, the message you wrote in the alert, will be display.

Attributes of <TABLE> Tag

Attributes	Explanation	Syntax
border	Add border to the table. (Takes value in pixel)	`<TABLE border="pixel">`
bordercolor	Specifies the color of table's border.	`<TABLE bordercolor="color_name|hex_number|rgb_number">`
frame	Specifies which part of the table's border will be visible. (Outer border)	`<TABLE frame="void|above|below|hsides| lhs|rhs| vsides|box|border">`
rules	Specifies which lines or rules to draw between rows and columns.	`<TABLE rules="none|groups|rows|cols|all">`

Attributes	Explanation	Syntax
cellpadding	Specifies the space (in pixel) between the edges of cells and its contents.	`<TABLE cellpadding="pixel">`
cellspacing	Specifies the space (in pixel) between two cells.	`<TABLE cellspacing="pixel">`
align	Specifies the alignment of the table in a web browser.	`<TABLE align="left|right|center">`
background	Used to set an image in background of the table.	`<TABLE background="path |image_name">`
bgcolor	Specifies the background color of the table.	`<TABLE bgcolor="color_name|hex_number|rgb_number">`
height	Set the height of the table. (In pixel or percentage)	`<TABLE height="pixel|percentage">`
width	Set the width of the table. (In pixel or percentage)	`<TABLE width="pixel|percentage">`
summary	Provides information about the table.	`<TABLE summary="text">`

Attributes of <TD> and <TH> Tags

Attributes	Explanation	Syntax
align	Used to align the table data.	`<TD|TH align= "left|right|center">`
height	Used to define the height of the cell.	`<TD|TH height=" pixel|percentage">`
width	Used to define the width of the cell.	`<TD|TH width="pixel|percentage">`
bgcolor	Specifies the background color of an individual cell.	`<TD|TH bgcolor="color_name|hex_number|rgb_number">`
background	Specifies the background image of an individual cell.	`<TD|TH background="path|image_name">`
rowspan	Used to span multiple rows, i.e. how many rows a cell should take.	`<TD|TH rowspan="number">`
colspan	How many columns a cell should span across.	`<TD|TH colspan="number">`
valign	Set the vertical alignment of that particular cell's content (when rowspan is more than one row).	`<TD|TH valign="top|bottom|middle">`

Attributes of <TR> Tag

Attributes	Explanation	Syntax
align	Specifies the alignment of the row content.	`<TR align= "left|right|center">`
bgcolor	Specifies the background color of an individual row.	`<TR bgcolor="color_name|hex_number|rgb_number">`
background	Specifies a background image for that particular row.	`<TR background="path|image_name">`
valign	Set the vertical alignment of the text of the cells inside the element.	`<TR valign="top|bottom|middle">`

Chapter Practice

Objective Questions

• Multiple Choice Questions

1. Which of these tags belong to table? [CBSE 2016]
   (a) <THEAD>,<BODY>,<TR>
   (b) <TABLE>,<HEAD>,<TFOOT>
   (c) <TABLE>,<TR>,<TD>
   (d) <TABLE>,<TR>,<TT>

Ans. (c) <TABLE>, <TR>, <TD> tags are used with table.

2. HTML tag for row is
   (a) <COLSPAN>
   (b) <TR>
   (c) <ROWSPAN>
   (d) <TD>

Ans. (b) HTML tag for row is <TR>, which is used to create a new row of data in a table.

3. Which tag is used to add columns in the table? [CBSE 2014]
   (a) <COLSPAN>
   (b) <TD>
   (c) <TR>
   (d) None of these

Ans. (b) <TD> tag is used to add columns in the table. TD stands for Table Data.

4. Which of the following tag gives a caption to the table?
   (a) <CAPTION>
   (b) <SUMMARY>
   (c) <FRAME>
   (d) None of these

Ans. (a) <CAPTION> tag is used to give caption to the table. It provides a short description of the table's purpose.

5. In order to add border to a table, border attribute is specified in which tag? [CBSE 2014]
   (a) <TH>
   (b) <TABLE>
   (c) <TD>
   (d) <TR>

Ans. (b) border attribute is specified in <TABLE> tag, which is used to add border to a table.

6. The attribute used to set the border color of a table is [CBSE 2011]
   (a) border
   (b) bordercolor
   (c) color
   (d) border color

Ans. (b) bordercolor is used to set the border color of a table. This attribute is used within <TABLE> tag.

7. The frame attribute contains ……… types of values.
   (a) 9
   (b) 3
   (c) 6
   (d) 4

Ans. (a) The frame attribute contains 9 types of values as : void, above, below, hsides, ths, rhs, vsides, box, border.

8. Which of the following is an attribute of <TABLE> tag? [CBSE 2011]
   (a) src
   (b) cellpadding
   (c) link
   (d) bold

Ans. (b) cellpadding is an attribute of <TABLE> tag. It is used to specify the space between the borders of the cell and contents of the cell.

9. Which one of the following is not an option for aligning data in a table? [CBSE 2016]
   (a) justify   (b) right   (c) left   (d) center

Ans. (a) justify is not option used for aligning data in a table.

10. Which attribute of the <TABLE> tag is used to set an image in the background of a table?
   (a) bgcolor
   (b) background
   (c) frame
   (d) rules

Ans. (b) background attribute of <TABLE> tag is used to set an image in the background of a table. It enables you to modify the background of your tables in HTML.

11. The attribute used to specify the background color of a table is [CBSE 2011]
   (a) color   (b) bgtable   (c) backcolor   (d) bgcolor

Ans. (d) bgcolor attribute is used to specify the background color of a table. By default, background color of a table is white.

12. The two common attributes of the <IMG> and the <TABLE> tags are [CBSE 2011]
   (a) src and height
   (b) height and width
   (c) border and src
   (d) they do not have any common attributes

Ans. (b) height and width are two common attributes of the <IMG> tag and the <TABLE> tag.

13. border, frame, cellspacing, cellpadding and align are the attributes of
    (a) <BODY> tag   (b) <IMG> tag
    (c) <TABLE> tag   (d) None of these

Ans. (c) border, frame, cellspacing, cellpadding and align are the attributes of <TABLE> tag.

14. Which of the following is not an attribute of <TABLE> tag?
    (a) border   (b) background (c) bgcolor   (d) src

Ans. (d) src (source) is not an attribute of <TABLE> tag.

15. In the <TD> tag, TD stands for
    (a) Table Data   (b) Time Date
    (c) Table Date   (d) None of these

Ans. (a) TD stands for Table Data, which specifies a cell or table data within a table.

16. Combining two or more cells in a table on a web page is called   **[CBSE 2011]**
    (a) merging   (b) spanning
    (c) combining   (d) None of these

Ans. (b) Combining two or more cells in a table on a web page is called spanning.

17. Choose the correct HTML code to right align the content inside a table cell.
    (a) `<TD align = "right">`
    (b) `<TD valign = "right">`
    (c) `<TD rightalign>`
    (d) `<TD right = "align">`

Ans. (a) `<TD align ="right">`
It is the correct HTML code to right align the content inside a table cell.

18. rowspan = n can be added to only which tag?
                            [CBSE 2014]
    (a) <HR>   (b) <TABLE>
    (c) <TD>   (d) <TR>

Ans. (c) rowspan = n can be added to only <TD> tag. rowspan attribute is used to span multiple rows.

19. Which attribute of <TD> tag is used to merge two or more columns to form a single column?
    (a) colspan   (b) cellspacing
    (c) cellpadding   (d) rowspan

Ans. (a) colspan attribute of <TD> tag is used to merge two or more columns to form a single column.

20. The ……… attribute helps to align data vertically in a single cell.
    (a) align   (b) valign
    (c) halign   (d) Both (b) and (c)

Ans. (b) valign attribute is used to align data vertically in a single cell.

21. In the <TH> tag, TH stands for
    (a) Table Heading   (b) Total Heading
    (c) Table Header   (d) All of these

Ans. (c) TH stands for Table Header, which is used to specify a table's header.

• Case Based MCQs

Direction *Read the case and answer the following questions.*

22. Tables can be divided into three portions as a head, a body and a foot. The head and foot are rather similar to headers and footers in a word processor document that remain the same for every page, while the body is the main content holder of the table.

The three elements for separating the head, body and foot of a table are as follows
    (i) <THEAD>   (ii) <TBODY>
   (iii) <TFOOT>

Browsers can use these elements to enable scrolling of the table body independently of the header and footer. Also, when printing a large table that spans multiple pages, these elements can enable the table header and footer to be printed at the top and bottom of each page.

  (i) Which tag indicates the header rows in a table?
    (a) <THEAD>   (b) <TBODY>
    (c) <TFOOT>   (d) All of these

  (ii) Which attribute(s) is/are contained in <TBODY> tag?
    (a) align   (b) bgcolor
    (c) valign   (d) All of these

 (iii) Which tag is used to indicate the footer rows?
    (a) <THEAD>   (b) <TBODY>
    (c) <TFOOT>   (d) None of these

 (iv) A table may contain several ………………… elements to indicate different pages or groups of data.
    (a) <THEAD>   (b) <TBODY>
    (c) <TFOOT>   (d) All of these

  (v) Which tag is used to show the main body of the table?
    (a) <THEAD>   (b) <TBODY>
    (c) <TFOOT>   (d) All of these

Ans. (i) (a) <THEAD> indicates that a group of rows are the header rows at the top of the table.
    (ii) (d) <TBODY> tag indicates that a group of rows are body rows or main body of the table. It contains align, bgcolor, valign attributes.

(iii) (*c*) <TFOOT> indicates that a group of rows are the footer rows at the bottom of the table.

(iv) (*b*) A table may contain several <TBODY> elements to indicate different pages or groups of data.

(v) (*b*) <TBODY> indicates that a group of rows are body rows or main body of the table.

PART 2
Subjective Questions

• Short Answer Type Questions

1. What is table? Name the basic commands for creating a table.

Ans. Tables are made up of rows and columns. In HTML, tables are used to display tabular data in web pages. The basic commands for creating tables are as follows:

Table tag <TABLE> </TABLE>

Row tag <TR> </TR>

Cell tag <TD> </TD>, <TH> </TH>

Caption tag <CAPTION> </CAPTION>

2. Write HTML code to display a table with border of 5px. **[CBSE 2016]**

Ans.
```
<HTML><BODY>
   <TABLE border = "5">
      <TR><TD>1</TD></TR>
      <TR><TD>2</TD></TR>
   </TABLE>
</BODY></HTML>
```

3. Differentiate between cellpadding and cellspacing in HTML table.

Ans. Differences between cellpadding and cellspacing are as follows

Cellpadding	Cellspacing
It is used for formatting purpose which specifies the space between the edges of the cells and also in the cell contents.	It is one also used for formatting purpose but it sets space between cells.
The general format of specifying cellpadding in HTML is as follows: `<TABLE width="100" border ="2" cellpadding="5">`	The general format of specifying cellspacing in HTML is as follows: `<TABLE width="100" border="2" cellspacing ="20">`
The default value of cellpadding attribute is 1.	The default value of cellspacing attribute is 2.

4. Name the attributes of <TABLE> tag, which are used for specifying its dimensions in a web page. **[CBSE 2016]**

Ans. width and height attributes of <TABLE> tag, which are used for specifying its dimensions in a web page. width and height are specified in terms of pixel or percentage of the browser window.

5. Explain the width attribute of <TABLE> tag.

Ans. The width attribute is used to set the absolute width of the table. The values in width attribute can be either in pixel or in percentage of the browser window.

e.g.
```
<TABLE width = "150">
    <TR><TD>Cell1</TD><TD>Cell2</TD></TR>
    <TR><TD>Cell3</TD><TD>Cell4</TD></TR>
</TABLE>
```

6. What is the function of summary attribute?

Ans. summary attribute of <TABLE> tag is used to provide the detailed information about a table. It enables a user to know the type of information that a table contains. It is useful to provide access to non-visual browsers, which are used by users with visual impairment.

e.g. `<TABLE summary="text">`

7. What is data cell? Name the <TABLE> tag, which is used as data cell.

Ans. The data cell defines a cell of a table that contains data. The table data cell is coded with <TD> tag of <TABLE> tag. Here, TD stands for Table Data. The content in the table data cell is normal and left-aligned by default.

8. Name the attributes that are used to do the following in HTML.

(i) Merge two or more rows

(ii) Change the background color of the cells in a table

(iii) Vertically align cell content

(iv) Merge two or more columns

Ans. (i) rowspan   (ii) bgcolor

(iii) valign   (iv) colspan

9. Name the attributes used for following.

(i) Setting the cell width

(ii) Setting cell's background image

(iii) Setting cell's background color

(iv) Changing the cell span

Ans. (i) width   (ii) background

(iii) bgcolor   (iv) rowspan and colspan

10. Which attributes can you use with <TABLE> tag but not with <TR> tag?

Ans. summary, rules, frame, border, cellpadding, cellspacing, height, width and bordercolor are the attributes that you can use with <TABLE> tag but not with <TR> tag.

11. Define the <TH> and <TR> tags. Are these two tags similar? If yes, how?

Ans. <TH> stands for Table Header. It is used to give headings to the various columns in our table. <TR> stands for Table Row. It is used to create a row in a table. <TH> and <TR> tags are not similar. <TH> tag is similar to <TD> tag. Since, <TH> tag also defines a data cell, which is taken as heading to the columns and the data is bold faced.

12. What is header cell? Name the <TABLE> tag, which is used as header cell.

Ans. The header cell specifies the header of the table and displays the content of a table in heading style. The content in the table header cell is rendered in bold and centered horizontally within the cell. The table header cell is coded with <TH> tag.

13. Mr. Ayush, Sports Captain of the school, has to display sequence of events of the upcoming Annual Sports Day on the school website. Help him in writing HTML code to create a table in HTML as shown in the given screenshot. **[CBSE 2019]**

Annual Sports Day-Sequence of Events		
8.00 AM-9.00 AM	9.00 AM-1:00 PM	1:00 PM-2:00 PM
Cultural Events	Track Events	Prize Distribution

Ans.
```
<HTML>
  <BODY>
    <TABLE border = "1">
      <TR>
<TH colspan ="3" align ="center"> ANNUAL

SPORTS DAY-SEQUENCE OF EVENTS</TH>
      </TR>
      <TR align ="center">
      <TD>8:00 AM - 9:00 AM</TD>
      <TD>9:00 AM-1:00 PM</TD>
      <TD>1:00 PM-2:00 PM</TD>
      </TR>
      <TR align ="center">
          <TD>CULTURAL EVENTS</TD>
          <TD>TRACK EVENTS</TD>
          <TD>PRIZE DISTRIBUTION</TD>
```

```
      </TR>
    </TABLE>
  </BODY>
</HTML>
```

14. What are the roles of rowspan and colspan attributes? Explain with suitable HTML example. **[Specimen Paper 2020]**

Ans. colspan attribute allows the user to stretch a cell to span multiple columns (merge two or more columns). rowspan attribute is used to span multiple rows (merge two or more rows).

```
e.g. <TABLE border = '1'>
      <TR>
      <TD> Row-1 Column-1 </TD>
      <TD colspan = "2"> Row-1 Column-2 and 3
                                        </TD>
      <TD rowspan = "2"> Row-1 and 2 Column-4
                                  </TD> </TR>
      <TR>
      <TD> Row-2 Column-1 </TD>
      <TD> Row-2 Column-2 </TD>
      <TD> Row-2 Column-3 </TD>
        </TR>
    </TABLE>
```

15. Saroj, a student of Class X, wants to represent a table in web page but she is unaware about the table tag. Explain her the role of <TH>, <TR> and <TD> tags. Write HTML code of a table and show the use of <TH>, <TR> and <TD> tags. **[Specimen Paper 2020]**

Ans. **<TR> tag** defines the table row which is used to create a new row of data in a table.

<TH> tag defines the table header which is used for specifying a table's header.

<TD> tag defines the table data which is used to specify a cell or table data within a table.

```
e.g. <TABLE>
      <TR>
          <TH>Name</TH>
          <TH>Subject</TH>
      </TR>
      <TR>
          <TD>Rahul</TD>
          <TD>Mathematics</TD>
      </TR>
      <TR>
          <TD>Muskan</TD>
          <TD>Science</TD>
      </TR>
    </TABLE>
```

• Long Answer Type Questions

16. Write the HTML code to create the exact table which is given below.   [CBSE 2011]

ADMNO	SNAME	NAME	DOB
1110	MANJIT	RANJIT	4-MAR-1998

Ans. The HTML code is

```
<HTML>
   <BODY>
   <TABLE border="3">
      <TR align="center" valign="middle">
         <TH> ADMNO </TH>
         <TH> SNAME </TH>
         <TH> NAME </TH>
         <TH> DOB </TH>
         </TR>
         <TR align="left" valign="middle">
         <TD> 1110 </TD>
         <TD> MANJIT </TD>
         <TD> RANJIT </TD>
         <TD> 4-MAR-1998 </TD>
      </TR>
   </TABLE>
   </BODY>
</HTML>
```

17. What is the use of <TR> tag in an HTML table? Give a suitable example.

Ans. The <TR> tag creates a table row in an HTML table. A table must have atleast one row and also, it can have as many table rows as you want. A table row is divided into table cells. A table must have atleast one table cell per table row.

e.g.
```
<HTML>
   <HEAD><TITLE> TR Tag </TITLE></HEAD>
   <BODY>
   <TABLE border = "1" cellpadding ="3">
   <TR>
      <TH> Head 1 </TH>
      <TH> Head 2 </TH>
      <TH> Head 3 </TH>
   </TR>
   <TR>
      <TD> A </TD>
      <TD> B </TD>
      <TD> C </TD>
   </TR>
   <TR>
      <TD> D </TD>
      <TD> E </TD>
      <TD> F </TD>
   </TR>
   </TABLE>
   </BODY>
</HTML>
```
Output

Head 1	Head 2	Head 3
A	B	C
D	E	F

18. Observe the following table and write the HTML code to generate it.   [CBSE 2013]

Period1	Period2
Math	Science
English	SST
Science	SST

Ans. The HTML code is
```
<HTML>
<BODY>
<TABLE cellpadding = "10" cellspacing="0"
border="1">
      <TR align = "center">
         <TH>Period1</TH>
         <TH>Period2</TH>
      </TR>
      <TR align = "center">
         <TD>Math</TD>
         <TD>Science</TD>
      </TR>
      <TR align="center">
         <TD>English</TD>
         <TD>SST</TD>
      </TR>
      <TR align="center">
         <TD>Science</TD>
         <TD>SST</TD>
      </TR>
   </TABLE>
   </BODY>
</HTML>
```

19. Write the HTML code to generate the following table on a web page with the contents and alignment exactly as shown below.   [CBSE 2011]

MOVID	MOVNAME	ACTORS
M001	HIT FACTORY	4

Ans. The HTML code is

```
<HTML>
    <BODY>
    <TABLE border="1" width = "400">
      <TR align="right">
        <TH>MOVID</TH>
        <TH>MOVNAME</TH>
        <TH>ACTORS</TH>
      </TR>
      <TR align="left">
        <TD>M001</TD>
        <TD>HIT FACTORY</TD>
        <TD>4</TD>
      </TR>
    </TABLE>
    </BODY>
</HTML>
```

20. Write the HTML code to generate the following table with the contents exactly in the same format as shown within the table. **[CBSE 2012]**

Shopping Mall			
Floor	No. of Toy Shops	No. of Food Shops	No. of Sports Shops

Ans. The HTML code is

```
<HTML><BODY>
    <TABLE border="1">
     <TR>
       <TH colspan="4" align="center">
       Shopping Mall</TH>
     </TR>
     <TR align = "center">
       <TD>Floor</TD>
       <TD>No. of Toy<BR>Shops</TD>
       <TD>No. of Food<BR>Shops</TD>
       <TD>No. of Sports<BR>Shops</TD>
     </TR>
    </TABLE>
    </BODY>
</HTML>
```

21. Observe the following table and write the HTML code to generate it. **[CBSE 2016]**

Activities	
Sr School	Maths Club
	Robotics Club
	Photography
Middle School	Gymnastic
	Yoga
	Computer Club
Primary School	Dance
	Vocal Music
	Swimming

Ans. The HTML code is

```
<HTML>
    <BODY><BASEFONT face="cambria">
    <TABLE border="1"  bordercolor="black"
    cellspacing="0" width="320">
    <CAPTION> Activities </CAPTION>
      <TR>
        <TD rowspan="3"> Sr School </TD>
        <TD> Maths Club </TD>
      </TR>
      <TR>
        <TD> Robotics Club </TD>
      </TR>
      <TR>
        <TD> Photography </TD>
      </TR>
      <TR>
        <TD rowspan="3">Middle School </TD>
        <TD> Gymnastic </TD>
      </TR>
      <TR>
        <TD> Yoga </TD>
      </TR>
      <TR>
        <TD> Computer Club </TD>
      </TR>
      <TR>
        <TD rowspan="3"> Primary School </TD>
        <TD> Dance </TD>
      </TR>
      <TR>
        <TD> Vocal Music </TD>
      </TR>
      <TR>
        <TD> Swimming </TD>
      </TR>
    </TABLE>
    </BODY>
</HTML>
```

22. Write names of two attributes each for the following tags. **[CBSE 2013]**

(i) <HR>   (ii) <BODY>

(iii) <IMG>   (iv) <TABLE>

(v) <A>

Ans.

	Tag	Attributes
(i)	<HR>	align, width
(ii)	<BODY>	bgcolor, text
(iii)	<IMG>	src, alt
(iv)	<TABLE>	border, rules
(v)	<A>	href, name

23. Write an HTML code to print the following table.

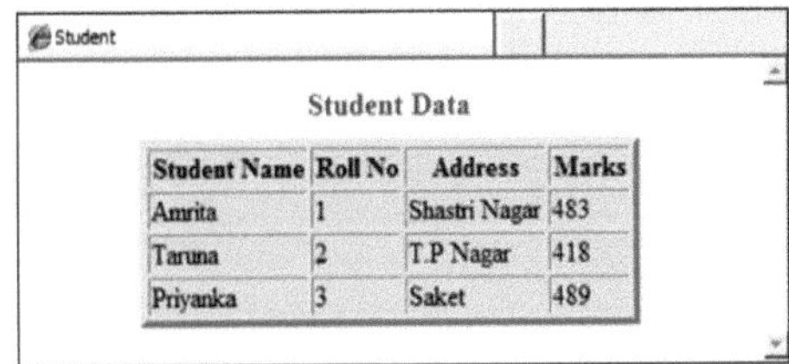

Note
- Background color of a table is pink.
- Caption of a table is in red color.

Ans. The HTML code is

```
<HTML>
  <HEAD>
   <TITLE>Student</TITLE>
  </HEAD>
  <BODY>
   <TABLE border="4" bgcolor="pink"
height="50%" width="70%"align="center">
<CAPTION>
<B>
   <FONT size="4" color="red">
   Student  Data
</FONT>
</B>
</CAPTION>
  <TR>
    <TH>Student Name</TH>
    <TH>Roll No</TH>
    <TH>Address</TH>
    <TH>Marks</TH>
  </TR>
  <TR>
    <TD>Amrita</TD>
    <TD>1</TD>
    <TD>Shastri Nagar</TD>
    <TD>483</TD>
  </TR>
  <TR>
    <TD>Taruna </TD>
    <TD>2</TD>
    <TD>T.P Nagar</TD>
    <TD>418</TD>
  </TR>
  <TR>
    <TD>Priyanka</TD>
    <TD>3</TD>
    <TD>Saket</TD>
    <TD>489</TD>
  </TR>
  </TABLE>
```

```
  </BODY>
</HTML>
```

24. Write the HTML code to generate the following web page.

Note The following points while generating the web page:
- Link color is green, active link color is blue and visited link color is red.
- Title of the page is "Eat healthy, live healthy".
- Heading of the page is maroon.
- Image used is "Restaurant.jpg".
- Caption of table is blue.
- Table border is blue and of size 2. **[CBSE 2011]**

Ans. The HTML code is

```
<HTML>
  <HEAD>
      <TITLE>Eat healthy, live healthy</TITLE>
  </HEAD>
  <BODY link="green" alink="blue" vlink="red">
  <CENTER>
  <H1>
  <FONT color="maroon">KHAO PIYO
              RESTAURANT </FONT>
  </H1>
  </CENTER>
  <IMG src="Restaurant.jpg"
align="right"height="255"
width="250">
  Collect Information for
  <UL>
  <LI> Menus </LI>
  <LI> Reservation </LI>
  <LI> Catering </LI>
  <LI></LI>
  </UL>
  <CENTER>
  <TABLE border="2" bordercolor="blue">
  <FONT color="blue">
  <CAPTION> Menus  available are </CAPTION>
  </FONT>
  <TR>
```

```
        <TD> 1 </TD> <TD> INDIAN </TD>
</TR>
<TR>
        <TD> 2 </TD> <TD> ITALIAN </TD>
</TR>
<TR>
<TD> 3 </TD> <TD> CONTINENTAL </TD>
</TR>
<TR>
        <TD> 4 </TD> <TD> THAI </TD>
</TR>
        </TABLE>
</CENTER>
<BR>
```
For further queries and reservation
Contact Us
```
</BODY></HTML>
```

25. Carefully study the web page given below. Identify 8 tags (structural as well as formatting tags) that have been utilised in creating this web page and write the usage of each of them.   **[CBSE 2012]**

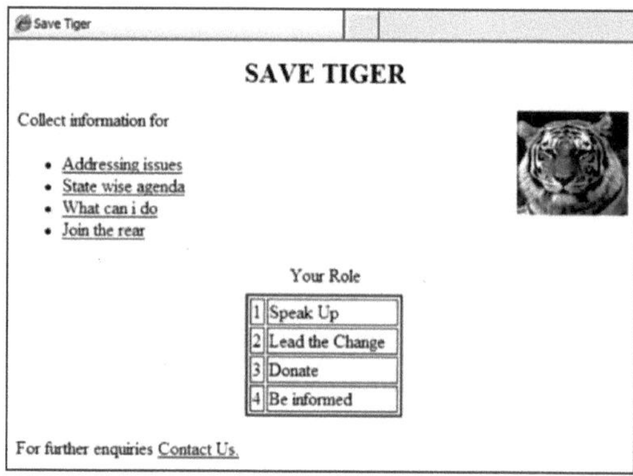

Ans. (i) **<TITLE>** to specify the title of the web page.

(ii) **<BODY>** contains all the content that is to be displayed on web page and all the various formatting and structural tags.

(iii) **<UL>** used to create an unordered list.

(iv) **<LI>** to specify the various list items in a list.

(v) **<CAPTION>** to provide caption to the table.

(vi) **<TABLE>** used to create table in HTML document.

(vii) **<TR>** stands for table row, used to create a table row.

(viii) **<TD>** stands for table data, helps to create cells in HTML table.

26. Observe the following web page and write HTML code to generate it.   **[CBSE 2014]**

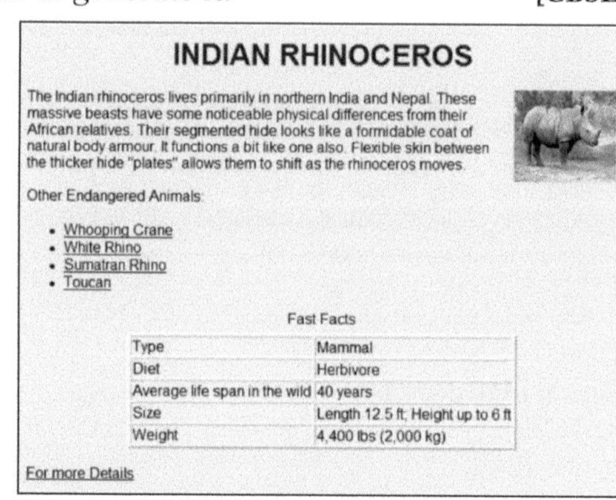

Note The following points while generating the web page:
- Background color of page is yellow.
- Link color is black and visited link color is green.
- Font style for the page is arial.
- Heading of the page is maroon.
- Image used is mainrhino.jpg.
- Table border is 2px.

Ans. The HTML code is
```
<HTML>
<BODY bgcolor="yellow" link="black"
vlink="green">
<BASEFONT face="arial">
<H1 align="center">
<FONT color="maroon">INDIAN
RHINOCEROS</FONT></H1>
<IMG src="mainrhino.jpg" align="right"
height="100" width="110">
```
The Indian rhinoceros lives primarily in northern India and Nepal. These massive beasts have some noticeable physical differences from their African relatives. Their segmented hide looks like a formidable coat of natural body armour. It functions a bit like one also. Flexible skin between the thicker hide "plates" allows them to shift as the rhinoceros moves.
```
<BR><BR>
```
Other Endangered Animals:
```
<UL>
<LI>
```
Whooping Crane
```
</LI>
<LI>
```
White Rhino
```
</LI>
<LI>
```

```
Sumatran Rhino
</LI>
<LI>
Toucan
</LI>
</UL>
<TABLE border="2" align="center">
<CAPTION>Fast Facts</CAPTION>
<TR><TD>Type</TD>
<TD>Mammal</TD>
</TR>
<TR>
<TD>Diet</TD>
<TD>Herbivore</TD>
</TR>
<TR>
<TD>Average life span in the wild</TD>
<TD>40 years</TD>
</TR>
<TR>
<TD>Size</TD>
<TD>Length 12.5 ft; Height up to 6 ft</TD>
</TR>
<TR>
<TD>Weight</TD>
<TD>4,400 lbs (2,000 kg)</TD>
</TR>
</TABLE>
<BR>
For more Details
</BODY>
</HTML>
```

Chapter Test

Multiple Choice Questions

1. Which of the following is used to specify the beginning of a table's row?
  (a) <TABLE>   (b) <TR>   (c) <ROW>   (d) <BEGIN>

2. The .... tag is used to specify the individual table data in a table.   [CBSE 2011]
  (a) <TR>   (b) <TD>   (c)<TH>   (d)<TABLE>

3. What is the correct HTML code to left align the content inside a table cell?
  (a) <TD valign = "left">   (b) <TD align = "left">
  (c) <TD left align>   (d) <TD left>

4. Which attribute tells, how many rows a cell should span?
  (a) colspan = n   (b) rowspan = n   (c) Both (a) and (b)   (d) None of these

5. colspan = n can be added to ...... tag.   [CBSE 2013]
  (a) <HR>   (b) <TABLE>   (c) <TD>   (d) <TR>

Short Answer Type Questions

6. Explain any four values for frame attribute of <TABLE> tag.

7. Write HTML code to display a table with border of 3 px.

8. Define the elements for separating the head, body and foot of a table in HTML.

9. Observe the following table and write the HTML code to generate it.

Sunday	Monday
Tuesday	Wednesday
Thursday	Friday

10. Explain the rowspan and colspan attributes.

Long Answer Type Questions

11. Write an HTML code to create the following table.

Roll Number	Name	Class
100	Amit	10 A
101	Ankit	10 B
102	Arnab	10 C
Footer 1	Footer 2	Footer 3

Note First row has green background.

12. Observe the following table and write the HTML code to generate it.   [CBSE 2014]

question	marks
1	2
	2
	5

Note First row has pink background.

13. Identify which of the following is a tag or an attribute?   [CBSE 2014]
  (i) link   (ii) table
  (iii) align   (iv) href

Answers

Multiple Choice Questions

  1. (b)   *2. (b)*   *3. (b)*   *4. (b)*   *5. (c)*

CHAPTER 04

Links and CSS in HTML

In this Chapter...

- Linking
- Sending E-Mail from a Browser (mailto)
- Embed Audio and Video in HTML Page
- Cascading Style Sheet (CSS)

Hyperlink is an interesting element within an HTML web page. It is a word or image that you can click on, to jump to another web page or within the same web page.

CSS stands for Cascading Style Sheets. It is a style sheet language which is used to describe the look and formatting of a document written in markup language.

Linking

A key feature of the HTML is its ability to link text and/or an image to another document or within a document. If you are on a web page and see the colored and/or an underlined text, it is a **hyperlink**. It is also known as **hypertext link** or just **link**. By default, color of a hyperlink is blue.

The main objectives of linking are as follows
   (i) To add more pages to the website and link them together.
   (ii) Using internal links (anchors) to save scrolling for visitors.
   (iii) To indirect the user to web page of different website.

In other words, hyperlinks are the links that carry user from one web page to another (within or on another website). It is activated by clicking on an underlined text or image. And, when the mouse pointer is brought over a hyperlink, the pointer changes to a hand. In HTML, links can be created by using < A > **anchor tag**. <A> tag is a container tag that means it requires a starting as well as ending tags.

To include an anchor in your document, you should do the following
   (i) Start the anchor tag with < A.
   (ii) Specify the document you are linking to, by entering the parameter href = "file name with extension".
   (iii) Place closing right angle bracket (>).
   (iv) Enter the text that will serve as the hypertext link after the opening <A> tag.
   (v) Enter the closing anchor tag </A>.

More precisely, it can be seen as

```
<A href ="mypage.html">My another page</A>
```

Here, it is noticeable that the final </A> tag is required. If it is not included, everything following that link will also be linked to another document, until the tag is closed.

Types of Linking

There are two types of linking in a web page, which are as follows

1. External Linking

This leads to a link that go to another website. In other words, it refers to a different page on a different website. When a user clicks on a hyperlink on a web page, user is directed on the location, which is specified in that hyperlink. To create an external link with <A> tag and its href attribute (to define URL of target document), a title attribute also needed.

href Attribute

The href stands for Hypertext REFerence. The href attribute is used to specify the URL of the target document. It is used to specify the destination of web page, which is linked. Notice, the pages on Internet should give a complete URL, i.e. alongwith http://.

e.g. To show external linking.

```
<HTML>
   <HEAD> <TITLE> Creating a Hyperlink </TITLE>
   </HEAD>
   <BODY> <H1> Look at the image </H1>
   <BR><IMG src ="D:\images.jpg"
      alt = "It is a beautiful picture">
      <A href = "http://www.google.com">
      Click Here </A> to get more flower images.
   </BODY>
</HTML>
```

Output

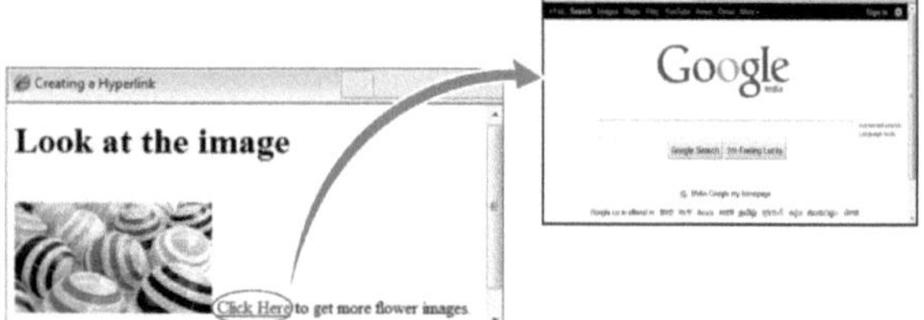

Images as Links

Images can also be used as hyperlinks. To create image as a link, following syntax is used

```
<A href = "URL"> <IMG src="image1.jpg"> </A>
```

e.g. To show image as link.

```
<HTML>
   <HEAD>
      <TITLE>Image as Link</TITLE>
   </HEAD>
   <BODY>
      <A href="http://en.wikipedia.org/wiki
      /Tweety">
      <IMG src="D:\Class10\computer
      \tweety1.jpg"></A>
   </BODY>
</HTML>
```

Output

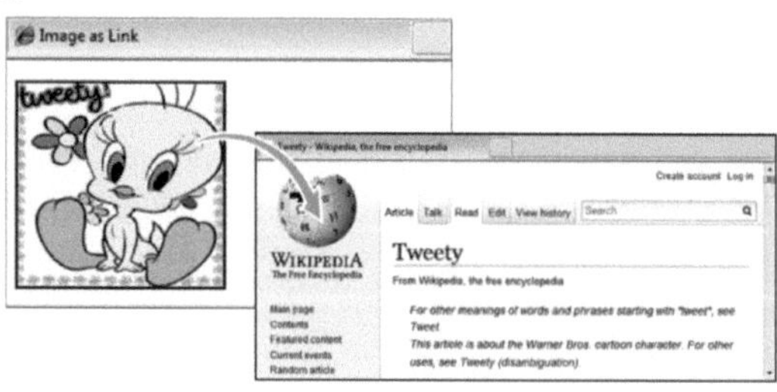

Listed Hyperlinks

It is noticeable that < A > tag can also be used for more complex task (as with images or with lists etc.),

e.g. To show listed hyperlinks.

```
<HTML>
   <HEAD> <TITLE> List </TITLE> </HEAD>
   <BODY> <H1> List </H1>
      <UL>
      <LI><A href="link1.html"><IMG src="F:
      \Fruits-wallpaper-91.jpg"
      align="middle" height="75" width="75">
      Fruit Chart </A></LI><BR><BR>
      <LI> <A href= "link2.html">
      <IMG src="F:\vegetable.jpg"
      align="middle" width="75" height="75">
      Vegetable Chart </A> </LI> </UL>
   </BODY>
</HTML>
```

Output

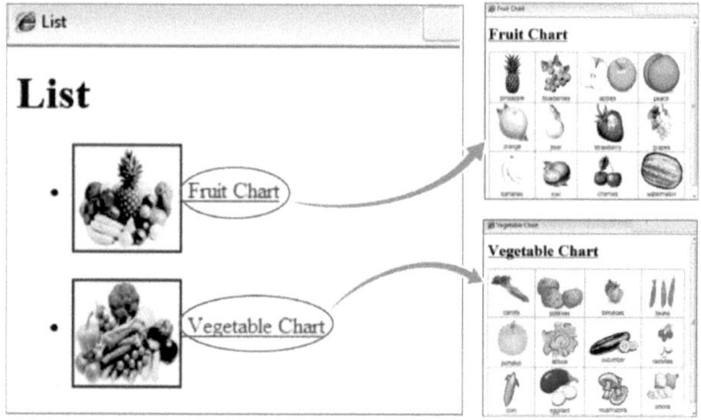

title Attribute

The title attribute of anchor <A> tag is used to specify the title of the document to which, we are linking. The value of the title attribute can be any string enclosed within double (or single) quotes. It is used for referencing an unlabeled resource (like an image or a non–HTML document). The value specified for this attribute appears as a tooltip when the mouse pointer is placed over the hyperlink. The title attribute can also be used by the browser, when adding the link to the user's hotlist.

e.g. To illustrate the use of title attribute.

```
<HTML>
   <HEAD><TITLE>Creating Hyperlink </TITLE></HEAD>
   <BODY>
      <A href ="http://www.google.com" title
      ="It is a hyperlink"> Click Here </A>
   </BODY>
</HTML>
```

Output

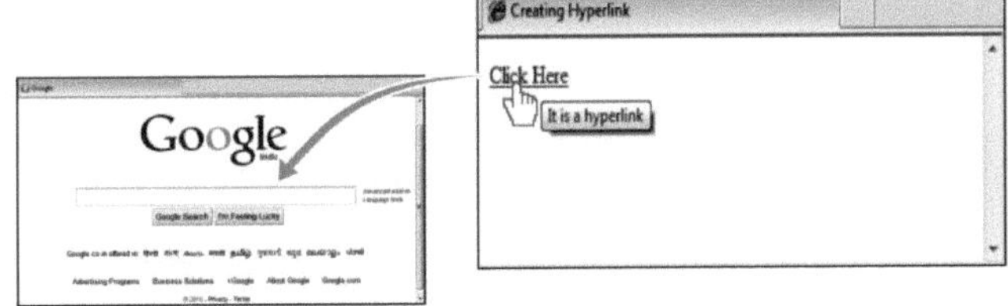

Output

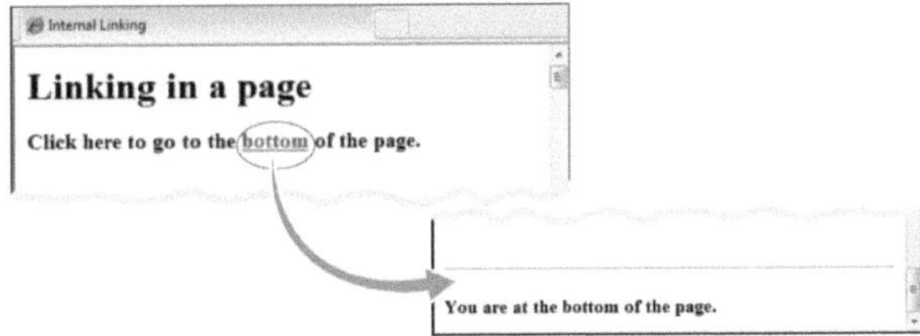

2. Internal Linking

This is a type of HTML linking that links pages within a single website, various sections of same document or different document.

Linking on the Same Web Page

To create an internal link, you need to use a pair of <A> tags. The first <A> tag is used to specify the name of the target location for identification purpose. It is known as **target fragment**. You can use the <A> tag with its name or id attribute to identify a fragment. This type of anchor is commonly called as **named anchor**.

The first step is to make the target fragment. The simple syntax to do so is written below

```
<A name ="aa"> Part A </A>
```

where, "aa" is the name of fragment/segment that you want to refer (like top, bottom etc.). The second <A> tag is used to create a link to the target fragment. The simple syntax to link to the target segment is written below

```
<A href = "#aa"> Click Here </A>
```

In the second <A> tag, the value of href attribute with # symbol is to be specified.

e.g. To show the internal linking in an HTML document.

```
<HTML>
   <HEAD><TITLE>Internal
Linking</TITLE></HEAD>
   <BODY>
      <H1>Linking in a page </H1>
      <H3>Click here to go to the
      <A href="#bottom">bottom</A>of the
      page.</H3>
         <BR><BR><BR><BR><BR><BR><BR><BR><BR>
         <BR><BR>
         <BR><BR><BR><BR><BR><BR><BR><BR>
         <BR><BR>
         <BR><BR><BR><BR><BR><BR><BR><BR><BR>
         <BR><BR>
      <A name="bottom"><H3> You are at the
      bottom of the page.</H3></A>
   </BODY>
</HTML>
```

Linking Sections of Different Web Pages

Internal linking enables us to link sections of different web pages also. It can be done by specifying the name of the web page and the section which is to be linked. To link two web pages, you first need name to the section by using name attribute of <A> tag that you want to link. Suppose, we need to link a section of HTML1.html to HTML2.html. Create a named anchor in HTML1.html.

The syntax is given below

```
<A name ="link"> Different Page </A>
```

After this, you have to write the code to refer to it, from web page HTML2.html. Following is the code to do so

```
<A href ="HTML1.html#link">
```

Here, HTML1.html is the name of HTML file to the section of which you want to link and # link is the segment name you want to link in that html file.

Significance of Linking

Links on a web page allow user to jump to another document. It is a very useful feature of HTML as when you click on a hypertext, it carries you to other document.

It enables the web page writer to refer to other documents and thus prevent the need of creating large document.

e.g. if you are reading an E-book, where many chapters are explained, if you want to read the last chapter of the book, then by using hyperlink, you can go to that chapter directly without scrolling down to whole book.

Sending E-Mail from a Browser (mailto)

Sending and receiving E-mails is the quickest and economical means of communication. The mailto attribute of <A> tag is used to serve the purpose of sending E-mails through a website. It enables E-mailing, which helps visitors to send feedback through the website.

The mailto value when used alongwith an E-mail address in href attribute of anchor tag, will create a link. When this link will be clicked, it will open default E-mail client. You can also add a header to E-mail sent from a mailto link. Using "?Subject = Subject line", we can add subject line of the E-mail window.

e.g. To illustrate the use of mailto function.

```
<HTML>
    <HEAD><TITLE> Mailto Attribute </TITLE></HEAD>
    <BODY>
        Send to <A href="mailto:job@someplace.com?
        Subject='Sent from ABC'">
        jobs@someplace.com </A>
    </BODY>
</HTML>
```

Output

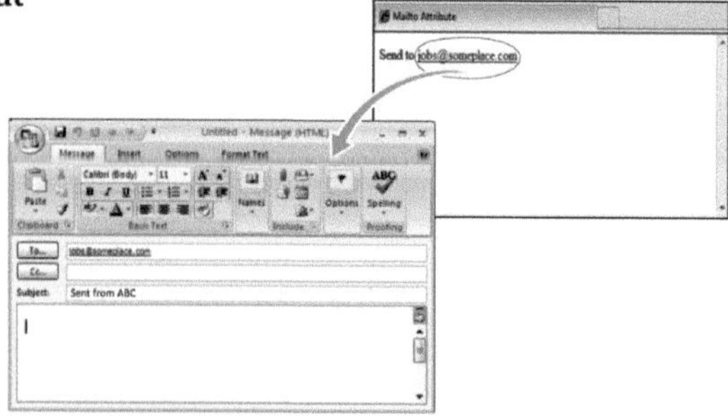

Embed Audio and Video in HTML Page

HTML allows us to create standards-based video and audio players that do not require the use of any plugins.

Embed Audio Element

The <AUDIO> element is used to embed sound content in HTML documents. It may contain one or more audio sources, represented using the src attribute. The <AUDIO> element defines an in-browser audio player. The audio player can provide a single piece of audio content. To specify the source file of the audio content, use one or more <SOURCE> elements inside the <AUDIO> element.

All <SOURCE> files should contain the same audio content, but in different file formats. The browser will select the first file format that it is able to play. If you are not going to provide multiple source file formats, you may indicate the source file in the src attribute, instead of in a separate <SOURCE> element.

Attributes of <AUDIO> tag

Attribute	Description
autoplay	This boolean attribute if specified, the audio will automatically begin to play back as soon as it can do so without stopping to finish loading the data.
autobuffer	This boolean attribute if specified, the audio will automatically begin buffering even if it's not set to automatically play.

Attribute	Description
controls	If this attribute is present, it will allow the user to control audio playback, including volume, seeking and pause/resume playback.
loop	This boolean attribute if specified, will allow audio automatically see back to the start after reaching at the end.
src	This attribute specifies the location (URL) of the audio file. This is optional, you may instead use the <SOURCE> element within the audio block to specify the audio to embed.
type	This attribute specifies the audio file standard type.

Most commonly used audio formats are ogg, mp3 and wav. You can use <SOURCE> tag to specify media alongwith media type and many other attributes. An audio element allows multiple source elements and browser will use the first recognised format.

e.g.

```
<HTML>
    <BODY>
        <AUDIO controls autoplay>
            <SOURCE src = "/html/audio.ogg"
                                type = "audio/ogg"/>
            <SOURCE src = "/html/audio.wav"
                                type = "audio/wav"/>
        Your browser does not support the <AUDIO>
        element.
        </AUDIO>
    </BODY>
</HTML>
```

Output

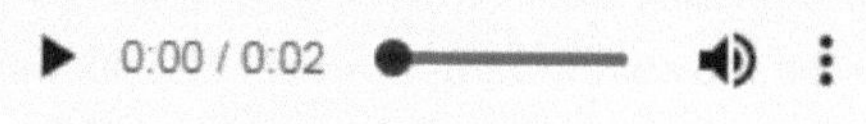

Embed Video Element

The <VIDEO> element allows us to embed video files into an HTML document, very similar to the way images are embedded. The HTML does not specify which video formats browser should support in the <VIDEO> tag, but most commonly used video formats are ogg, mpeg4.

Attributes of <VIDEO> tag

Attribute	Description
autoplay	This boolean attribute if specified, the video will automatically begin to play back as soon as it can do so without stopping to finish loading the data.
autobuffer	This boolean attribute if specified, the video will automatically begin buffering even if it's not set to automatically play.
controls	If this attribute is present, it will allow the user to control video playback, including volume, seeking and pause/resume playback.

Attribute	Description
height	This attribute specifies the height of the video display area in pixels.
width	This attribute specifies the width of the video display area in pixels
src	The URL of the video to embed. This is optional, you may instead use the <SOURCE> element within the video block to specify the video to embed.
type	This attribute specifies the video file standard type.

e.g.

```
<HTML>
    <BODY>
        <VIDEO width = "300" height = "200" controls
                                    autoplay>
        <SOURCE src = "/html/foo.ogg"
                                type = "video/ogg"/>
        <SOURCE src = "/html/foo.mp4"
                                type = "video/mp4"/>
        Your browser does not support the <VIDEO>
        element.
        </VIDEO>
    </BODY>
</HTML>
```

Output

Cascading Style Sheet (CSS)

It is a style sheet language used for describing the presentation of a document written in a markup language. CSS is designed primarily to enable the separation of document content from document presentation, including aspects such as the layout, colors and fonts. This separation can improve content accessibility, provide more flexibility and control in the specification of presentation characteristics, enable multiple HTML pages to share formatting by specifying the relevant CSS in a separate .css file, and reduce complexity and repetition in the structural content such as semantically insignificance tables that were widely used to format pages before consistent CSS rendering was available in all major browsers.

CSS makes it possible to separate presentation instructions from the HTML content in a separate file or style section of the HTML file. For each matching HTML element, it provides a list of formatting instructions.

Syntax

A CSS rule-set consists of a selector and a declaration block.

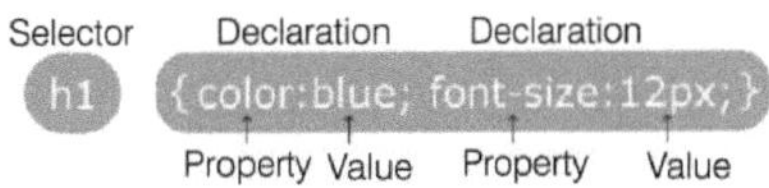

The selector points to the HTML element that you want to style.

The declaration block contains one or more declarations separated by semicolons.

Each declaration includes a CSS property name and a value that separated by a colon.

A CSS declaration always ends with a semicolon and declaration blocks are surrounded by curlybraces.

e.g.

```
P
{
    color : red;
    text-align: center;
}
```

Declaration of CSS in HTML is as follows

```
P
{
    color:red;
    text-align: center;

}
BODY
{
    background-color:yellow;
}
H1
{
    font-size: 36pt;
}
H2
{
    color:blue;
}
P
{
    margin-left:50px;
}
```

Above code is Style_01.css file. CSS file declares as follows in which HTML document save as CSS_Example_01.html.

```
<HTML>
    <HEAD>
        <LINK rel= "stylesheet" type = "text/css" href
        = "Style_01.css"/>
    </HEAD>
    <BODY>
        <H1> This header is 36 pt</H1>
        <H2> This header is blue </H2>
        <P>This paragraph has a left margin of
        50 pixels </P>
```

```
    </BODY>
</HTML>
```

Output

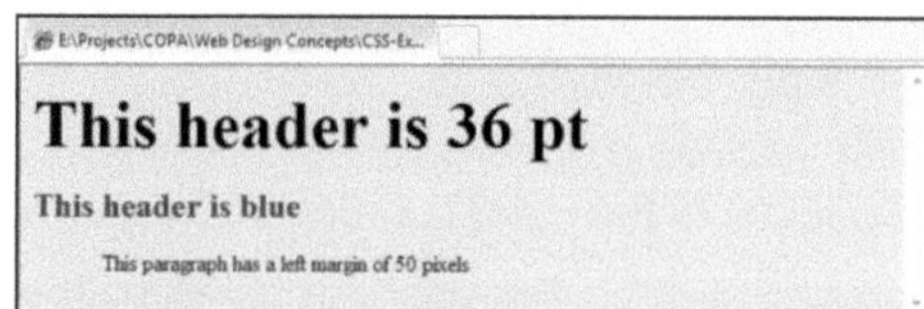

Property Value of CSS

Following table defines the property value of CSS.

Property	Description	Syntax
color	Sets the color of a text.	`color: color|` `initial|inherit;`
background -color	Sets the background color for HTML document.	`background-color:` `color|transparent|` `initial|inherit;`
border-style	This property sets the style of an element border. This property can have from one to four values.	`border-style:` `none|hidden|dotted` `|dashed;`
margin	The CSS margin properties are used to create space around elements, outside of any defined borders. CSS has properties for specifying the margin for each side of an element; margin-top, margin-right, margin-bottom, margin-left.	`margin: length|` `auto|initial|` `inherit;`
height	This property sets the height of an element.	`height:` `auto|length|` `initial|inherit;`
width	This property sets the width of an element.	`width:auto|value|` `initial|inherit;`
outline	An outline is a line that is drawn around elements, outside the borders, to make the element "stand out".	`outline:` `outline-width|` `outline-style|` `outline-color;`
font-family	It is used to set the font type of an HTML element.	`font-family:` `family-name|` `generic-family|` `initial|inherit;`
font-size	This property sets the size of a font.	`font-size: font` `size value;`
font-style	It is used to specify the font-style of an HTML element.	`font-style:` `normal|` `|italic|initial|` `inherit;`
float	It is a CSS property written in CSS file or directly in the style of an element. The float property defines the flow of content.	`float:` `none|left|right` `|initial|inherit;`

Property	Description	Syntax
text-align	This property specifies the horizontal alignment of text in an element.	`text-align:` `left|right` `|center|justify;`
padding	The padding of an element is the space between its content and its border	`padding: length|` `initial|inherit;`

id Selector and class Selector

The id selector uses the id attribute of an HTML element to select a specific element.

An id should be unique within a page, so the id selector is used if you want to select a single and unique element. To select an element with a specific id, write a hash (#) character, followed by the id of the element.

Below code save as CSS_Example_02. html

```
<HTML>
    <HEAD>
        <STYLE type = "text/css">
        #para1
        {
            font-size : 36pt;
            text-align: center ;
            color : blue :
        }
        </STYLE>
    </HEAD>
    <BODY>
        <P id="para1"> Hello World ! </P>
        <P> This paragraph is not affected
            by the style. </P>
    </BODY>
</HTML>
```

Output

In which, style rule will be applied to the HTML element with id= "para1".

The class selector selects elements with a specific class attribute.

To select elements with a specific class, write a period (.) character, all HTML elements with class = "center" will be red and center-aligned.

In below code, HTML document save as CSS_Example_03. html.

```
<HTML>
    <HEAD>
        <STYLE type= "text/css">
```

```
      .center
      {
         text-align: center;
      }
      </STYLE>
   </HEAD>
   <BODY>
      <H1 class= "center">
         Arihant COMPUTER BOOKS </H1>
      <P class = "center"> Arihant Computer
                    Books for POLYTECHNIC</P>
   </BODY>
   </HTML>
```

Output

As class, id should not be start from any number. Many browsers such as Internet Explorer, Mozilla Firefox do not support it.

Inserting CSS

In HTML, CSS can be inserted in various ways, which are as follows

1. External Style Sheet

With an external style sheet, you can change the look of the website by changing just one file.

Each page must include a reference to the external style sheet file inside the <LINK> element. The <LINK> element goes inside the <HEAD> section.

e.g.
```
<HEAD>
   <LINK rel = "stylesheet" type ="text/css"
   href = "mystyle.css">
</HEAD>
```

An external style sheet can be written in any text editor. The style sheet file must be saved with a .css extension.
```
HR
{ color : white; }
H1
{ font-size = 40;}
P
{ margin-left : 20px; }
BODY {background-image : url("E:\Projects\COPA\Web
Design Concepts\colorful.jpg");}
```

Above code is a file as Style_02.css.

e.g.

In HTML code, which is save as CSS_Example_04.html.
```
<HTML>
   <HEAD>
```

```
      <LINK rel ="stylesheet" type = "text/css"
      href ="Style_02.css"/>
      <TITLE> Arihant BOOKS </TITLE>
   </HEAD>
   <BODY>
      <H1> Arihant Books </H1>
      <P>A wide range of books for school curricula,
polytechnic, competitive and recruitment
examinations are published by <B> Arihant
Publications India Ltd. </B> </P>
      <HR>
      For any query e-mail at info@arihantbooks.
com and crm@arihantbooks.com
      or dial+91-11-40546380
   </BODY >
</HTML>
```

Output

2. Internal Style Sheet

An internal style sheet may be used if one single page has a unique style. Internal styles are defined within the <STYLE> element, inside the <HEAD> section of an HTML page.

e.g

HTML code save as CSS_Example_05.html.
```
<HTML>
   <HEAD>
      <STYLE type = "text/css">
      HR
      {color : white ;}
      H1
      {font-size = 40;}
      P
      {margin-left:20px;}
      BODY
      {background-image : url ("E :/Projects/COPA
      /Web Design Concepts/colorful.jpg")}
      </STYLE>
      <TITLE>Arihant BOOKS</TITLE>
   </HEAD>
   <BODY>
      <H1>Arihant Books </H1>
```

```
<P> A wide range of books for school curricula,
polytechnic, competitive and recruitment
examinations are published by <B> Arihant
Publications India Ltd. </B></P>
<HR>
```

For any query e-mail at info@arihantobooks.com and crm@arihantbnooks.com or dial +91-11-40546380

```
</BODY>
</HTML>
```

Output

3. Inline Style

An inline style may be used to apply a unique style for a single element.

To use inline styles, add the style attribute to the relevant element. The style attribute can contain any CSS property. e.g.

HTML code save as CSS_Example_06.html.

```
<HTML>
    <HEAD>
        <STYLE type = "text/css">
            HR {color : white; }
            H1 {font-size = 40;}
            P {margin-left: 20px;}
        BODY
        {background-image: url ("E :\Projects\COPA\Web
        Design Concepts\colorful.jpg"); }
        </STYLE>
        <TITLE> Arihant BOOKS </TITLE>
    </HEAD>
    <BODY>
```

```
<H1>Arihant Books </H1>
<P> A wide range of books for school curricula,
polytechnic, competitive and recruitment
examinations are published by <B> Arihant
Publications India Ltd. </B> </P>
<HR style = "color: black"> For any query
```
e-mail at info@arihantbooks.com and crm@arihantbooks.com or dial +91-11-40546380
```
</BODY>
</HTML>
```

Output

4. Multiple Style Sheets

If some properties have been defined for the same selector (element) in different style sheets, the value from the last read style sheet will be used.

e.g. H3 selector for properties value of external style sheet in HTML document are as follows

```
H3
{
color:red;
text-align:left;
font-size: 8pt;
}
```

H3 selector for internal style sheet are as follows:

```
H3
{
    text-align:right; font-size:20pt ;
}
```

If the internal style is defined after the link to the external style sheet, the H3 elements will be

```
color : red ; text-align: right; font-size : 20pt;
```

Chapter Practice

Objective Questions

• Multiple Choice Questions

1. .... is the default color of a hyperlink.
(a) Red   (b) Blue   (c) Green   (d) Black
Ans. (*b*) By default, color of a hyperlink is blue.

2. Which of the following is not the attribute of <A> tag?   **[CBSE 2019]**
(a) name   (b) title
(c) href   (d) src
Ans. (*d*) SRC is not the attribute of <A> tag.

3. The tag used in HTML to link a web page with other web page is   **[CBSE 2013]**
(a) <A>   (b) <H>   (c) <U>   (d) <L>
Ans. (*a*) <A> anchor tag is used in HTML to link a web page with other web page. It is a container tag that means it requires a starting as well as ending tags.

4. Which tag tells, where a link starts?   **[CBSE 2014]**
(a) <L>   (b) <START>
(c) <A>   (d) None of these
Ans. (*c*) <A> tag specifies that a link starts, in which, href attribute creates a hyperlink.

5. Which command should be used to link a page with HTML page?   **[CBSE 2013]**

```
(a) <A link = "page.htm"></A>
(b) <A href = "page.htm">page</A>
(c) <A connect = "page.htm"></A>
(d) <A attach = "page.htm"></A>
```

Ans. (*b*) `<A href="page.htm">page</A>`
In which <A> tag creates a hyperlink and href attribute is used to specify the URL of the target document.

6. With which code, you can make an image works as hyperlink?   **[CBSE 2016]**

```
(a) <A href = "URL">Text</A>
(b) <A href="ABC.html"><IMG src =
    "graphic.gif">Click Here</A>
(c) <A ref=mailto:<IMG src
    ="graphic.gif">Click Here</A>
```

(d) None of the above
Ans. (*b*) With `<A href="ABC.html"><IMG src="graphic.gif">Click Here</A>` image works as hyperlink.

7. To create a hyperlinked image,
(a) the <IMG> tag should be within <A> tag
(b) the <A> tag should be within <IMG> tag
(c) the <IMG> tag should be before the <A> tag
(d) the <IMG> tag should be after the <A> tag
Ans. (*a*) The <IMG> tag should be within <A> tag to create hyperlinked image.

8. Is it possible to link within the current page?
(a) No   (b) Only in framesets
(c) Yes   (d) Cannot say
Ans. (*c*) Yes, it is possible to link within the current page, which is called internal linking.

This is a type of HTML linking that links pages within a single website, various sections of same document or different documents.

9. For internal linking, section names are provided by .... attribute of <A> tag.
(a) title   (b) href
(c) name   (d) None of these
Ans. (*c*) For internal linking, section names are provided by name attribute of <A> tag.

10. ...... attribute of the <A> tag is used to name a section in a web page to create an internal link.
(a) href   (b) name
(c) align   (d) link
Ans. (*b*) name attribute of <A> tag is used to name a section in a web page to create an internal link.

11. Which of the following is used to send E-mails through a website?
(a) tomail   (b) mailto
(c) Both (a) and (b)   (d) None of these
Ans. (*b*) mailto attribute is used to send E-mails through a website.

This function is used in href which creates a mail link upon clicking at which the mail software gets opened.

12. Choose the correct syntax to create an E-mail link.

[CBSE 2014]

```
(a) <A href = "abc@xyz.com">
(b) <A href = "mailto:abc@xyz.com">
(c) <mail = "abc@xyz.com">
(d) <A mail = "abc@xyz.com">
```

Ans. (b) `<A href ="mailto:abc@xyz.com">`
This code is used to create an E-mail link.

13. Which attribute of <AUDIO> element is used to give the URL of the audio to embed?

(a) controls (b) type   (c) src   (d) loop

Ans. (c) src attribute of <AUDIO> element is used to give the URL of the audio to embed.

14. ………… is designed primarily to enable the separation of document content from document presentation.

(a) HTML   (b) CSS
(c) CS   (d) None of these

Ans. (b) CSS (Cascading Style Sheet) is designed primarily to enable the separation of document content from document presentation, including aspects such as layout, colors and fonts.

15. Which property of CSS is used to set the font type of an HTML element?

(a) font-size (b) font-style   (c) font-family (d) float

Ans. (c) font-family property of CSS is used to set the font type of an HTML element.

16. In which of the following, selector hash (#) character is used?

(a) id   (b) class
(c) Both (a) and (b)   (d) None of these

Ans. (a) To select an element with a specific id, write an hash (#) character followed by the id selector.

An id should be unique within a page, so the id selector is used, if you want to select a single and unique element.

17. With an ……… you can change the look of the entire website.

(a) external style sheet   (b) internal style sheet
(c) inline style   (d) None of these

Ans. (a) With an external style sheet, you can change the look of the entire website by changing just one file.

• Case Based MCQs

Direction *Read the case and answer the following questions.*

18. Rahul is an expert of web page designing. He is mostly used CSS to design web pages, from which he saves his time. His younger brother Sonu does not understand the logic for saving time and space, then Rahul help him to know the importance of CSS.

CSS is designed primarily to enable the separation of document content from document presentation, including aspects such as the layout, colors and fonts. This separation can improve content accessibility, provide more flexibility and control in the specification of presentation characteristics, enable multiple HTML pages to share formatting by specifying the relevant CSS in a separate .css file, and reduce complexity and repetition in the structural content such as semantically insignificance tables that were widely used to format pages before consistent CSS rendering was available in all major browsers.

(i) The full form of CSS is

(a) Cascading Style Sheet
(b) Cascading Sheet Style
(c) Cascade Style Sheet
(d) Cascadation Style Sheet

(ii) CSS rule set consists of

(a) selector   (b) declaration
(c) Both (a) and (b)   (d) None of these

(iii) ……. points to the HTML element that you want to style.

(a) Selector   (b) Declaration
(c) ID   (d) None of these

(iv) A CSS declaration always ends with a

(a) dot   (b) colon   (c) semicolon   (d) hash

(v) Which of the following is/are property value of CSS?

(a) Color   (b) Margin
(c) Height   (d) All of these

Ans. (i) (a) The full form of CSS is Cascading Style Sheet. CSS is designed primarily to enable the separation of document content from document presentation, including aspects such as the layout, colors and fonts.

(ii) (c) A CSS rule set consists of a selector and a declaration block.

A selector points to the HTML element that you want to style.
The declaration block contains one or more declarations separated by semicolons.

(iii) (a) A selector points to the HTML element that you want to style.

e.g.

```
                    declaration
h1   {color  :  blue; font-size : 12px; }
     ↑       ↑         ↑
  selector property   value
```

(iv) (c) A CSS declaration always ends with a semicolon. Each declaration includes a CSS property name and a value that separated by colon.

(v) (*d*) The property value of CSS are color, margin, height, width, outline, float, padding, font-family, font-size,font-style, text-align etc.

19. Karan created a web page in which he wants to add audio clip to make web page more interesting. For this, he asked his teacher for help. The HTML <AUDIO> element is used to embed sound content in documents. It may contain one or more audio sources, represented using the src attribute. The <AUDIO> element defines an in-browser audio player. The audio player can provide a single piece of audio content. The browser will select the first file format that it is able to play. If you are not going to provide multiple source file formats, you may indicate the source file in the src attribute, instead of in a separate <SOURCE> element.

(i) <AUDIO> tag is used in
   (a) <HTML> tag
   (b) <BODY> tag
   (c) <HEAD> tag
   (d) <TITLE> tag

(ii) Which of the following options is/are attribute(s) of <AUDIO> tag?
   (a) autoplay   (b) src
   (c) type   (d) All of these

(iii) What is /are the attribute(s) of <SOURCE> tag?
   (a) src   (b) type
   (c) Both (a) and (b)   (d) height

(iv) This attribute specifies the location of the audio file.
   (a) loop   (b) src
   (c) type   (d) controls

(v) Most commonly used audio format(s) is/are
   (a) ogg   (b) mp3
   (c) wav   (d) All of these

Ans. (i) (*b*) <AUDIO> tag is used in <BODY> tag.

```
<HTML>
  <BODY>
    <AUDIO controls autoplay>
      <SOURCE src="/html/audio.ogg"
              type = "audio/ogg/">
    </AUDIO>
  </BODY>
</HTML>
```

(ii) (*d*) Attributes of <AUDIO> tag are autoplay, src, type, autobuffer, controls and loop.

(iii) (*c*) The attributes of <SOURCE> tag are src and type.

```
e.g. <SOURCE src ="/html/audio.wav" type
="audio/wav"/>
```

(iv) (*b*) src attribute specifies the location (URL) of the audio file. This is optional, you may instead use the <SOURCE> element within the audio block to specify the audio to embed.

(v) (*d*) Most commonly used audio formats are ogg, mp3 and wav. An audio element allows multiple source elements and browser will use the first recognised format.

PART 2
Subjective Questions

• Short Answer Type Questions

1. Explain the need of linking between web pages.

Ans. Linking between different web pages is required, as when we create websites, different html files (web pages) are created. These files contain different modules and cannot be open individually. If we link between them, the website becomes more productive and informative.

2. How is external linking different from internal linking?   **[CBSE 2004, 05]**

Ans. External link is a type of linking that goes to another website. It is a linking of two different documents. While, internal linking is a type of linking that links pages within a single website, various sections of same document or different documents.

3. Explain the given command
```
<A href ="wild.html">Click Here  for wild
animals  </A>
```
    [CBSE 2006]

Ans. In this command, anchor <A> tag and its href attribute is included. The text (Click Here for wild animals) will appear underlined and indicates that clicking the text activates the hypertext link. The address of the referenced document can be specified by an absolute or a relative URL.

Thus, "wild.html" is an URL or web page address and Click Here for wild animals is the hyperlinked text.

4. Name the attributes of <A> tag which are used for internal linking in a web page.   **[CBSE 2014, 13]**

Ans. The attributes of <A> tag which are used for internal linking in a web page as follows
(i) **href** is used to specify the URL of the segment the link goes to.
(ii) **name** gives the name to the segment.

5. Gaurav, a web designer in a company named "International Designers" has just created a web page in which different sections of the web page are linked and can be traversed by clicking on the text given as "Top", "Middle" and "Bottom". Is the internal linking or external linking and why?

Additionally tell him about the suitable tag and its attribute(s) to open another web page named 'second.html' by clicking on the text "Next". **[CBSE 2018]**

Ans. It is internal linking because links pages are within a single website, various sections of same document or different documents.

To open another web page, user will be need to use external linking with <A> tag and href attribute.

Suitable code to open web page named 'Second.html' <A href="second.html "> Next </A>

6. Write the HTML code to create a link for school.jpg located at C:\. **[CBSE 2014]**

Ans.
```
<HTML>
   <BODY>
      <A href = "C:\school.jpg">Image</A>
   </BODY>
</HTML>
```

7. Write an simple HTML code to show an example of internal linking.

Ans.
```
<HTML>
   <HEAD><TITLE>Internal Linking</TITLE>
   </HEAD>
   <BODY>
      <H1> It is <A name ="top">top</A>
      of the page </H1>
      <BR><BR><BR><BR><BR><BR><BR><BR><BR>
      <BR>
      <BR><BR><BR><BR><BR><BR><BR><BR><BR>
      <BR>
      <BR><BR><BR><BR>
      <H1><A href ="#top">Top</A></H1>
   </BODY>
</HTML>
```

8. What is the purpose of mailto function?

Ans. The mailto function is used to send E-mail messages to multiple recipients. For this, we only need to type the E-mail address of the recipients in the same link separated by commas.

9. Write an HTML code to show the use of mailto function.

Ans.
```
<HTML>
   <HEAD>
      <TITLE> Use of mailto </TITLE>
   </HEAD>
   <BODY>Send your views to
      <A href= "mailto:aaa_rr@gmail.com">
      aaa_rr@gmail.com</A>
   </BODY>
</HTML>
```

10. Write the HTML code to send an E-mail to abc@xyz.com from your web page. **[CBSE 2013]**

Ans.
```
<HTML>
   <BODY>
      <A href="mailto:abc@xyz.com">abc @xyz.com</A>
   </BODY>
</HTML>
```

11. Explain the cascading style sheet.

Ans. Cascading Style Sheet referred to as CSS, is a simple design language intended to simplify the process of making web pages presentable. CSS handles the look and feel part of a web page using CSS, you can control the color of the text, the style of fonts, the spacing between paragraphs, layout designs etc. CSS is easy to learn and understand but it provides powerful control over the presentation of an HTML document. Most commonly, CSS is combined with the markup languages HTML or XHTML.

12. Explain id selector in CSS.

Ans. id selector is used to apply the style to an element based on the id of an element.
e.g.
```
#elementid
{
color : #FFFFFF;
}
```
In the above code, all the elements having id. "elementid" will have the color white.

13. Write a code to display the text "Contact Us" should be linked with admin@taj.com E-mail id.

Ans.
```
<HTML>
<BODY>
<A href = "mailto:admin@taj.com"> Contact
Us </A>
</BODY>
<HTML>
```

14. Write a code to link www.google.com page with text Click Here and also show that title as "It is a hyperlink".

Ans.
```
<HTML>
<BODY>
<A href = "http ://www.google.com"
title = "It is a hyperlink"> Click Here
</A>
</BODY>
</HTML>
```

15. Define margin property of CSS.

Ans. The CSS margin properties are used to create space around elements, outside of any defined borders. CSS has properties for specifying the margin for each side of an element; margin-top, margin-right, margin-bottom, margin-left.

16. Explain class selector in CSS.

Ans. The class selector selects elements with a specific class attribute. To select elements with a specific class, write a period (·) character, all HTML elements with class = "center" will be red and center aligned.

17. Write about the following attribute of <AUDIO> tag.

(i) autobuffer   (ii) loop

(iii) type

Ans. (i) **autobuffer** This boolean attribute if specified, the audio will automatically begin buffering even if it is not set to automatically play.

(ii) **loop** This boolean attribute if specified, will allow audio automatically see back to the start after reaching at the end.

(iii) **type** This attribute specifies the audio file standard type.

18. Differentiate between internal CSS and external CSS.

Ans. Internal CSS are the ones that we can write within the same file, i.e. the HTML code and CSS code are placed in the same file.

While external CSS are that we can write in a separate file than the html code, i.e. the HTML file is separate and CSS file is separate.

• Long Answer Type Questions

19. What is the use of external style sheet? Explain its advantages and disadvantages.

Ans. With an external style sheet, you can change the look of the entire website by changing just one file. Each page must include a reference to the external style sheet, file inside the <LINK> element.

The <LINK> element goes inside the <HEAD> section. An external style sheet can be written in any text editor. The style sheet file must be saved with a .css extension.

The advantages of external style sheet are as follows

(i) With the help of external style sheets, the styles of numerous documents can be organised from one single file.

(ii) In external style sheets, classes can be made for use on numerous HTML element types in many forms of the site.

(iii) In complex contexts, methods like selector and grouping can be implemented to apply styles.

The disadvantages of external style sheet are as follows

(i) An extra download is essential to import style information for each file.

(ii) The execution of the file may be delayed till the external style sheet is loaded.

(iii) While implementing style sheets, we need to test web pages with multiple browsers in order to check compatibility issues.

20. Write the code using CSS to display following output.

Reaction of Magnesium with Hydrochloric Acid

The equation for the reaction is:
Magnesium+Hydrochloric Acid=Magnesium Chloride+Hydrogen
$Mg(s)+2HCL(aq)=Mgcl_2(ag)+H_2(g)$

Ans.

```
<HTML>
<HEAD>
    <STYLE type = "text/css">
    #para1
    {
    font-size: 10pt;
    text-align: center;
    color: blue;
    }
</STYLE>
</HEAD>
<BODY>
    <H2 id = "para1">Reaction of
    Magnesium with Hydrochloric Acid</H2>
    <B> The equation for the reaction
    is:</B><BR>
    Magnesium+Hydrochloric Acid =
    Magnesium Chloride + Hydrogen <BR>
    Mg(s)+2HCL(aq>=Mgcl<SUB>2</SUB>
    (ag)+H<SUB>2</SUB>(g)
</BODY>
</HTML>
```

21. Write an HTML code to display the following output.   [CBSE 2006]

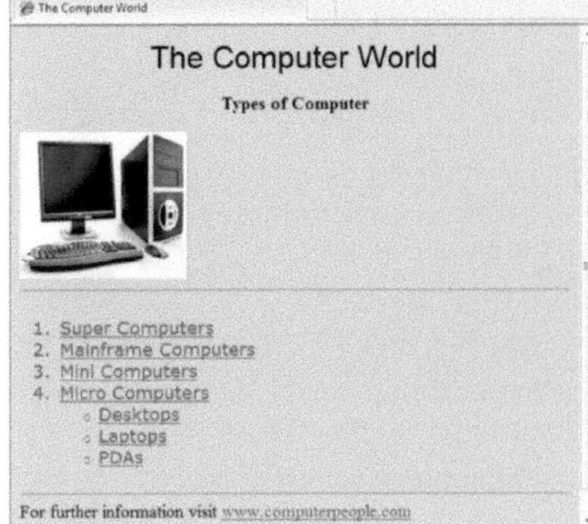

Consider the following points while writing the code

(i) Title of the page is "The Computer World".

(ii) Background color of the page is "Yellow".

(iii) Active link color is Green and Visiting link color is Red.

(iv) All font face in the page is Verdana but heading is in Arial and Black.

(v) Image is from the file "computer.jpg".

(vi) Use horizontal rule wherever required.

(vii) Use ordered and unordered lists wherever required.

(viii) The pages are linked as follows

Super Computers	`Super.html`
Mainframe Computers	`Main.html`
Mini Computers	`Mini.html`
Micro Computers	`Micro.html`
Desktops	`Desk.html`
Laptops	`Laptop.html`
PDAs	`PDA.html`

Note You can use any other attributes that are not mentioned above to produce a similar output.

Ans. The HTML code is

```
<HTML>
  <HEAD>
      <TITLE>The Computer World</TITLE>
  </HEAD>
  <BODY bgcolor="yellow" alink ="green"
  vlink="red">
    <FONT face="arial"color="black">
    <H1>
    <CENTER>The Computer World</CENTER>
    </H1>
    </FONT>
    <BASEFONT face="verdana">
      <P align="center"><B>
      Types of Computer
      </B></P>
      <IMG src="computer.jpg">
      <HR>
      <OL type="1">
      <LI><A href="Super.html">
      Super Computers </A></LI>
      <LI><A href="Main.html">
        Mainframe Computers</A></LI>
      <LI><A href="Mini.html">
        Mini Computers</A></LI>
      <LI><A href="Micro.html">
        Micro Computers</A></LI>
      <UL>
      <LI><A href="Desk.html">Desktops
      </A></LI>
      <LI><A href="Laptop.html">Laptops
      </A></LI>
      <LI><A href="PDA.html">PDAs
      </A></LI>
```

```
      </UL> </OL> <HR>
      <FONT size="4">
      For further information visit
      <A href="www.computerpeople.com">
      www.computerpeople.com</A>
      </FONT>
  </BODY>
</HTML>
```

22. Write an HTML code to display the following output.   **[CBSE 2005]**

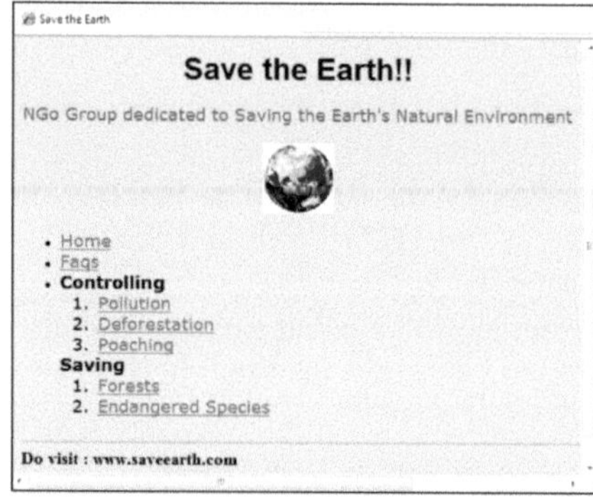

Consider the following points while writing the code

(i) Title of the page is "Save the Earth!!".

(ii) The background color of the page is Silver.

(iii) The font used for heading is "Arial", size is 6 and color is Black.

(iv) The sub heading is in "Verdana" font, font size is 4 and color is Brown.

(v) Rest of the text is in "Verdana" font, font size 4 and black color.

(vi) Image used is from file "Main.jpg".

(vii) The links are provided in an unordered list with ordered list used in between.

(viii) The pages are linked as follows

Home	`Home.html`
Faqs	`Faq.html`
Pollution	`Poll.html`
Deforestation	`Defores.html`
Poaching	`Poach.html`
Forests	`Forest.html`
Endangered Species	`Specie.html`

(ix) The categories 'Controlling' and 'Saving' in the unordered list are not linked to any page.

(x) The width and height of horizontal line is 820 and 80, respectively.

Note You can use any other attributes that are not mentioned above to produce a similar output.

Ans. The HTML code is

```
<HTML>
  <HEAD>  <TITLE> Save the Earth </TITLE>
  </HEAD>
  <BODY bgcolor ="silver">
    <H1>
    <FONT face="arial" color="black"
    size="6">
    <CENTER>Save the Earth!! </CENTER>
    </FONT>
    </H1>
    <FONT face="verdana" color="brown"
     size="4">
    <P align="center">NGo Group dedicated
to Saving the Earth's Natural
Environment</P>
    </FONT>
    <FONT face ="verdana" color="black"
    size="4">
    <CENTER>
    <IMG src ="Main.jpg">
    </CENTER>
    <UL type = "disc">
    <LI>
    <A href="Home.html">Home</A>
    </LI>
    <LI>
    <A href="Faq.html">Faqs</A>
    </LI>
    <LI>
    <B> Controlling </B>
    </LI>
    <OL type="1">
    <LI>
    <A href="Poll.html">
Pollution</A>
    </LI>
    <LI>
    <A href="Defores.html">
Deforestation</A>
    </LI>
    <LI>
    <A href="Poach.html">
Poaching</A>
    </LI>
    </OL>
    <LI>
    <B> Saving </B>
    </LI>
    <OL type="1">
    <LI>
    <A href="Forest.html">
Forests</A>
```

```
    </LI>
    <LI>
    <A href="Specie.html">
Endangered Species</A>
    </LI>
    </OL>
    </UL>
    </FONT>
    <HR noshade width="820"
    height="80" size="2">
    <B><FONT size="4">Do visit:
www.saveearth.com</FONT></B>
  </BODY>
</HTML>
```

23. Sushila, a web designer working with Global Designers, is supposed to design a web page shown below   **[CBSE 2019]**

Write the HTML code to design the above shown web page considering the specifications as given below

(i) Background color of the page should be pink and all the hyperlinked text should be green in color.

(ii) Image named "taj.jpg" should be placed in the centre of the web page.

(iii) Heading "The Taj Mahal" should be first level of the heading and underlined.

(iv) Paragraph should have following formatting styles applicable

Color-Blue

Size-5

Font style-Times New Roman

(v) At the bottom of the page, "Contact Us" text should be linked with admin@taj.com E-mail id.

Ans.
```
<HTML>
  <HEAD>
    <TITLE>Taj Mahal</TITLE>
  </HEAD>
  <BODY bgcolor="pink">
  <CENTER>
  <IMG src="taj.jpeg" height="100"
                width="150">
```

```
<H1><U>The Taj Mahal</U></H1>
</CENTER>
<P><FONT color="blue"size="5"
face="Times New Roman">
The Taj Mahal is a world famous white marble<BR>
monument located on the Yamuna river bank in <BR>
the Indian historical city of Agra.
</FONT>
</P>
<FONT color = "green">
<A href = "mailto:admin@taj.com">
Contact Us</A>
</FONT>
</BODY>
</HTML>
```

24. Observe following output and write HTML code to generate it. **[CBSE 2018]**

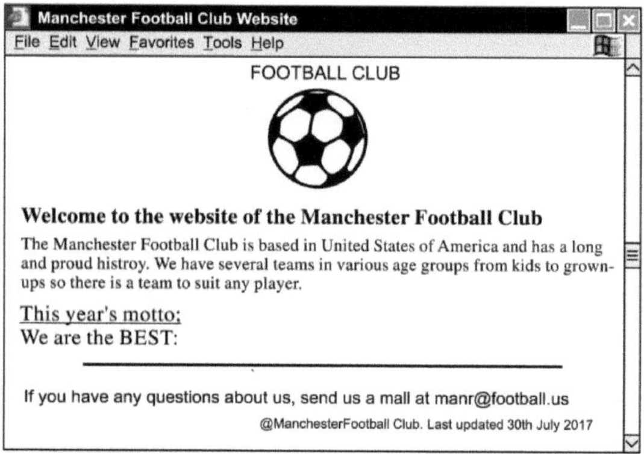

Consider the following points while generating the web page

(i) The title of the page is "FOOTBALL CLUB"

(ii) The heading is blue color

(iii) Font of entire document is arial

(iv) Image used is "football.jpeg"

(v) The page is linked to:
Proud history to "history.html"

(vi) Bottom message is of size 2.

Ans. The code is
```
<HTML>
<HEAD><TITLE>FOOTBALL CLUB</TITLE></HEAD>
<BODY>
<FONT face="arial" size="3">
<H1 align="center"><FONT
color="blue">FOOTBALL CLUB</FONT></H1>
<CENTER><IMG src="football.jpg" height="150"
width="150"></CENTER>
<H3>Welcome to the website of the Manchester Football
Club</H3>
```

```
<P>The Manchester Football Club is based in United States of
America and has a long <BR>
and <A href="history.html">proud history</A>.
We have several teams in various age groups from kids to
grown-<BR>ups so there is a team to suit any player. <BR><BR>
<U>This year's motto:</U><BR>
We are the BEST:<BR>
<HR size="3" noshade size ="75%">
<FONT size="2"><B>If you have any questions about us,
send us a mail at manr@football.us</B></FONT><BR>
<H5 align="right">
<IMG src="copy.jpg" height="20"
width="30">Manchester Football Club. Last updated
30<SUP>th</SUP>July 2017</H5>
</FONT>
</BODY>
</HTML>
```

25. Carefully study the web page given below. Identify 10 tags (structural as well as formatting tags) that have been utilised in creating this web page and write the usage of each of them.

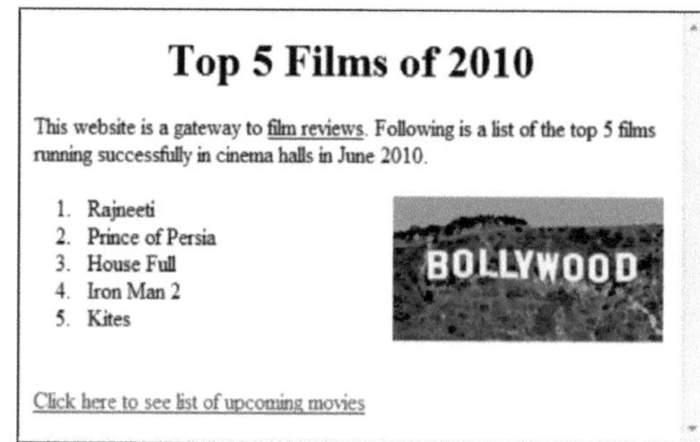

Ans. Following tags are used

(i) **<HTML>** Container of all the HTML elements. Tells the browser that it is dealing with an HTML document.

(ii) **<BODY>** It defines the document's body. It contains all the necessary contents of HTML document that is to be displayed on web browser.

(iii) **<H1>** Top level of heading.

(iv) **<CENTER>** Used to centralise a segment of text to be displayed.

(v) **<P>** It is used to define the paragraph.

(vi) **<OL>** To insert an ordered list in the web page.

(vii) **<LI>** It is used to indicate a list item as contained in an ordered.

(viii) **
** Break line tag is used to move all the text/image that follows the tag to the next line.

(ix) **<IMG>** This tag is used to insert the desired image into the web page.

(x) **<A>** Anchor tag is used to create the hyperlink.

26. Observe the following web page and write HTML code to generate it. **[CBSE 2013]**

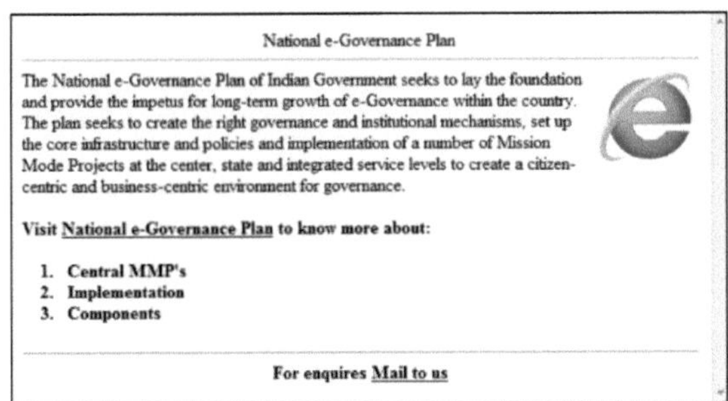

Note The following points while generating the web page:
  (i) Background color of page is yellow.
  (ii) Link color is black and visited link color is green.
  (iii) Font style for the page is arial.
  (iv) Heading of the page is maroon.
  (v) Image used is gov.jpeg.
  (vi) Text color of the paragraph is red.
  (vii) Link for 'National e-Governance Plan' is nation.html.
  (viii) E-mail id for bottom message is abc@xyz.com.

Ans. The HTML code is

```
<HTML>
  <BODY bgcolor="yellow" link ="black"
  vlink="green">
  <BASEFONT face = "arial">
  <CENTER>
  <FONT color="maroon"><H1>
  National e-Governance Plan</H1>
  </FONT></CENTER><HR>
  <P> <FONT color="red">
  <IMG src="gov.jpeg" alt="gov"
  align="right">
```

The National e-Governance Plan of Indian Government seeks to lay the foundation and provide the impetus for long-term growth of e-Governance within the country. The plan seeks to create the right governance and institutional mechanisms, set up the core infrastructure and policies and implementation of a number of Mission Mode Projects at the center, state and integrated service levels to create a citizen-centric and business-centric environment for governance.

```
  </FONT></P>
  <BR>
  <B>Visit<A href ="nation.html">
  National e-Governance  Plan</A>  to know
  more about:<BR>
  <OL type ="1">
  <LI>Central MMP's</LI>
  <LI>Implementation</LI>
  <LI>Components</LI>
  </OL></B><HR>
  <CENTER>For enquires
```

```
  <A href="mailto:abc@xyz.com">Mail to us
  </A>
  </CENTER>
  </BODY>
</HTML>
```

27. Write the HTML code to display the following output. **[CBSE 2011]**

Note The following points while generating the web page:
  (i) Title of the page should be "Dubai Tourism".
  (ii) The heading text "WELCOME TO DUBAI" is in arial font and is of maroon color.
  (iii) The horizontal lines below the heading are 5 pixels thick and of red color.
  (iv) Image used in the page is burj.jpg.
  (v) The bulleted list contains links as specified below
      • The text Morning is a link to the web page "morning.html"
      • The text Evening is a link to the web page "evening.html"

Ans. The HTML code is

```
<HTML>
  <HEAD>
    <TITLE>Dubai Tourism</TITLE>
  </HEAD>
  <BODY>
    <CENTER>
    <H1>
    <FONT face="arial" color="maroon">
      WELCOME TO DUBAI</FONT>
    </H1>
    </CENTER>
    <HR width=80% size="5" color="red"
    noshade>
    <HR width=60% size="5" color="red"
    noshade>
    <P>
    <FONT size="5">
      Enjoy the world of pure travel masti
    </FONT>
    <IMG src="burj.jpg" align="bottom"
    width="110">
    </P>
```

The following is alist of major tourist attractions in Dubai:`<BR><BR>`

```
    <UL type="disc">
```

```
<LI>
<A href="morning.html">
Morning</A>
- Dolphinarium and Palm Dubai
</LI>
<LI>
<A href="evening.html">
Evening</A>
- Ski Dubai and Cruise
</LI>
</UL>
<CENTER>
        For enquires write at dubai@gmail.com
</CENTER>
</BODY>
</HTML>
```

28. Neha is creating a web page on which hyperlinks are used. Her friend Niya does not know about the term hyperlink. Neha told her about hyperlink.

A web page can contain various links that take you directly to other pages and even specific parts of a given page. These links are known as hyperlinks.

Hyperlinks allow visitors to navigate between websites by clicking on words, phrases, and images. Thus, you can create hyperlinks using text or images available on a web pages.

Answer the following questions.

[Specimen Paper 2020]

(i) What is a hypertext link or hyperlink?

(ii) Give the name and the syntax of the HTML tag which is used for creating a hypertext link.

(iii) Neha wants to display a 'Click Here' message on her web pages which, when clicked, opens a new web page 'Chapter2.html'. Write the syntax of the HTML command she should use.

(iv) On the same web page, Neha whose E-mail is neha@xyz.com, wants to display a 'Contact us' message which when clicked open the E-mail program and allows the user to send a mail to Neha. Write the syntax of the HTML command she should use.

(v) Explain the use of the target attribute in the hypertext link tag.

Ans. (i) A hyperlink is an element in HTML document that links to either another portion of the document or to another document altogether. On web pages, hyperlinks are usually colored purple or blue and are sometimes underlined.

Hyperlinks can assume any of the following appearances.

(a) Text

(b) Images

(c) URLs

(d) Controls (e.g. button)

(ii) Name : Anchor tag

Syntax

```
<A href = "link address"> Hyperlink Text
</A>
```

(iii)
```
<A href = "Chapter2.html"> Click Here
</A>
```

(iv)
```
<A href = "mailto : neha@xyz.com">
Contact us </A>
```

(v) target attribute specifies where to open the linked document when the link is clicked.

Chapter Test

Multiple Choice Questions

1. Symbol used in href for linking to the section in the same document.
  (a) #   (b) @
  (c) ?   (d) None of these

2. The float property of a CSS defines the
  (a) content   (b) text
  (c) flow of content   (d) None of these

3. .... property of CSS specifies the horizontal alignment of text in an element.
  (a) float   (b) width
  (c) text-align   (d) padding

4. .... uses the id attribute of an HTML element to select a specific element.
  (a) class selector   (b) id selector
  (c) Both (a) and (b)   (d) None of these

5. Which of the following linking allows a link to another section on the same or different web pages?
  (a) Internal   (b) External
  (c) Inline   (d) Outline

Short Answer Type Questions

6. Write the HTML code to create a link for nature. jpg located at E:\.

7. Write the HTML code to send an E-mail to meerut@123.com.

8. What is the use of <VIDEO> element?

9. Define the following attributes of <VIDEO> tag.

  (i) src   (ii) autobuffer

10. What is the difference between href and src attributes?

11. Observe the following code and give the output

```
<HTML>
<HEAD>
<STYLE type="text/CSS">
#para1
{
        font-size:36 pt;
        text-align:center;
        color:blue;

}
</STYLE>
</HEAD>
<BODY>
<P id="para1">Hello World!!!</P>
<P>This paragraph is not affected by the style</P>
</BODY>
</HTML>
```

Long Answer Type Questions

12. Observe the following web page and write the HTML code to generate it

Note The following points while generating the web page
  (i) Title of the page is Educational Psychology.
  (ii) Font face of the heading should be "antiqua".
  (iii) Image used in the page is the file "eppic.jpg".
  (iv) Text color of the main heading should be blue.
  (v) Use links as:
   • For Intelligent Tutoring System as "Psycho1.htm"
   • For Educational Technology as "Psycho2.htm"
   • For Cooperative Learning as "Psycho3.htm"

13. Write the code to generate the following web page.

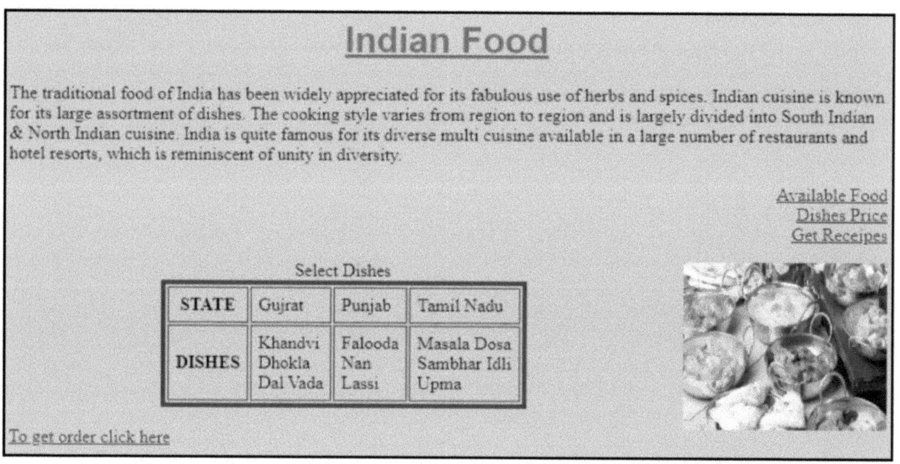

Note The following points while generating the web page
  (i) Title of the page is "Indian Food".
  (ii) Link color is blue, vlink color is brown and alink color is pink.
  (iii) Font face of heading is "arial".
  (iv) The color of the heading of the page is green.
  (v) Image used as food1.jpg.
  (vi) Table border is 4px and border color is maroon.
  (vii) Use link as:
   • For Available Food as F1.html
   • For Dishes Price as F2.html
   • For Get Recipes as F3.html
  (viii) E-mail id for bottom message "To get order click here" as inquiry@abc.com.

14. Write the code to generate the following web page.

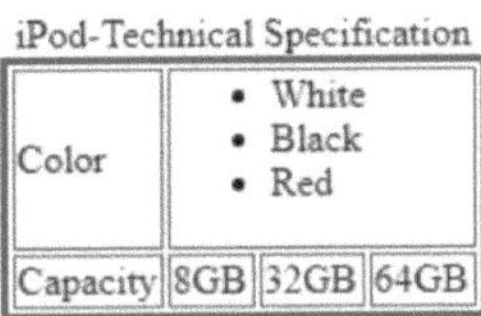

Note The following points while generating the web page.

(i) Title of the page is "iPod Touch".

(ii) Font face of the heading should be "arial".

(iii) Image used in the page is the file "ipod1.jpg" stored in the same directory.

(iv) Text color of the main heading should be blue.

(v) Link color of the page should be red.

(vi) Table border is 3px and border color is green.

(vii) Use links as:
   * For Select Colors as SC1.html
   * For Advance Features as SC2.html
   * For Client Query as SC3.html

(viii) E-mail id for bottom message is appleipod@xyz.com.

Answers

Multiple Choice Questions

1. (a)   *2. (c)*   *3. (c)*   *4. (b)*   *5. (a)*

CBSE Term II
Computer Applications X

Practice Papers
1-3

Practice Paper 1*
(Solved)

General Instructions

■ **Time :** 2 Hours
■ **Max. Marks :** 25

1. There are 8 questions in the question paper. All questions are compulsory.
2. Question no. 1 is a Case Based Question, which has five MCQs. Each question carries one mark.
3. Question no. 2-6 are Short Answer Type Questions. Each question carries 2 marks.
4. Question no. 7-8 are Long Answer Type Questions. Each question carries 5 marks.
5. There is no overall choice. However, internal choices have been provided in some questions. Students have to attempt only one of the alternatives in such questions.

*** As exact Blue-print and Pattern for CBSE Term II exams is not released yet. So the pattern of this paper is designed by the author on the basis of trend of past CBSE Papers. Students are advised not to consider the pattern of this paper as official, it is just for practice purpose.**

1. Direction *Read the following passage and answer the questions that follows*

It is the communication protocol for the Internet. It defines the rules, computers must follow to communicate with each other over the Internet. The TCP/IP is a protocol used with E-mail transmission. Infact, it is a set of protocol, i.e. TCP and IP.

The TCP/IP is a protocol which is responsible for finding path for the destination. It also splits the message into several datagrams, if it does not fit in one datagram. Therefore, these datagrams are sent through different alternate paths towards the destination. The TCP makes sure that the datagram arrives at the destination correctly.

IP (Internet Protocol) used by the Internet for transferring messages from one machine to another. The messages are sent in the form of packets. IP defines the packet structures that encapsulate the data to be delivered. It also defines addressing methods that are used to label the datagram with source and destination format.

(i) The full form of TCP/IP is
   (a) Transmission Control Protocol/Internet Protocol
   (b) Transfer Control Protocol/Internet Protocol
   (c) Transmission Control Protocol/Internal Protocol
   (d) Transfer Control Protocol/Internal Protocol

(ii) What is protocol?
   (a) A set of rules applicable for sending an E-mail
   (b) A set of rules applicable for a network
   (c) A set of rules applicable for social media
   (d) A set of rules applicable for good netiquette

(iii) Which of the following protocol is used for delivering data from the source to the destination?

    (a) TCP   (b) IP   (c) SMTP   (d) ARPANET

(iv) Which communication protocol is used by Internet?

    (a) TCP/IP   (b) WWW   (c) HTML   (d) W3C

(v) Which part of TCP/IP is responsible for dividing a file or message into very small parts, at the source computer?

    (a) TCP   (b) IP   (c) Both (a) and (b)   (d) All of these

2. What is the use of POP3 protocol?

Or List some benefits of E-learning.

3. Write HTML code to display a table with border of 4 px and table caption is Table.

4. What is website? Also, give its example.

5. Write the code to display following table.

Annual Function		
9 : 00 AM- 11 : 00AM	11 : 00 AM- 1 : 00 PM	2 : 00 PM- 3 : 00 PM
Singing	Dancing	Prize Distribution

Or Write about the following attributes of <VIDEO> tag.

    (i) autobuffer   (ii) width   (iii) type\

6. What is MODEM?

Or Mr. Lal owns a factory which manufactures automobile spare parts. Tell him about the web page and also suggest the advantages of having a web page for this factory.

7. What is search engine? How to locate sites using search engine?

Or Distinguish between web browser and web server.

8. Write the code to generate the following web page

Painting Exhibition in India

Painting is basically an art of applying paint, pigment, color or other elements with the help of brush, knives, sponges or airbrushes to any surface. Under our roof you will find large assortments of unmatched paintings with creative style statement. Paintings can be done on the surfaces of walls, paper and many more to deliver creative art style of the painter. The broad spectra of paintings can be easily classified into contemporary paintings, nature paintings, modern paintings and many more according to the painter's art style.

Available Paintings

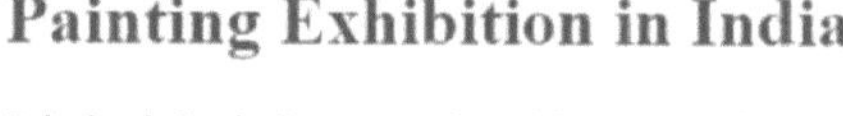

INDIAN	PAINTING		
	NAME	QTY	PRIZE
	Oil Painting	4	3000
	Glass Painting	2	5000
	Canvas	2	1000

For more inquiry Click here

The following points while generating the web page.

    (i) Title of the page is "Painting Exhibition in India".

    (ii) The heading text color should be red.

    (iii) Font style for the page is "calibri".

(iv) vlink color should be red and alink color should be orange.

(v) Table border is 3px and border color is blue.

(vi) Image used in the page is paint1.jpg.

(vii) E-mail id as inquiry@abc.com for bottom message as "For more inquiry Click here".

Or Explain linking with its types.

Explanations

1. (i) (*a*) The full form of TCP/IP is Transmission Control Protocol/Internet Protocol. It is the communication protocol for the Internet.

(ii) (*b*) Protocol refers to the set of rules applicable for a network. It allows the setting up of a valid connection, communication and data transferring between two computing end points.

(iii) (*b*) IP (Internet Protocol) is used for delivering data from source to destination. These data or messages are sent in the form of packets.

(iv) (*a*) TCP/IP is the communication protocol is used by Internet. It defines the rules, computers must follow to communicate with each other over the Internet.

(v) (*a*) TCP stands for Transmission Control Protocol. It is responsible for dividing a file or message into very small parts, at the source computer.

2. POP3 (Post Office Protocol Version 3) is a standard mail protocol used to receive E-mails from a remote server to a local E-mail client. It allows you to download E-mail messages on your local computer and read them even when you are offline. When you use POP3 to connect to your E-mail account, messages are downloaded locally and remove from the E-mail server.

Or

Some benefits of E-learning are as follows

(i) It is self-paced.

(ii) It can work on any location and anytime.

(iii) Online computer based courses are available.

(iv) Reduces travel time and travel cost.

3.
```
<HTML> <BODY>
<TABLE border = "4">
<CAPTION> Table </CAPTION>
<TR> <TD> One </TD> </TR>
<TR> <TD> Two </TD> </TR>
</TABLE>
</BODY> </HTML>
```

4. A group of related web pages that follow the same theme and are connected together with hyperlinks is called a website. A website displays related information on a specific topic. Each website is accessed by its own address known as URL.

e.g. http://www.carwale.com is a website.

5.
```
<HTML>
<BODY>
<TABLE border = "2">
<TR>
<TH colspan ="3" align = "center"> Annual
                          Function </TH>
</TR>
<TR align = "center">
<TD> 9:00 AM-11:00 AM </TD>
<TD> 11:00 AM-1:00 PM </TD>
<TD> 2:00 PM-3:00 PM </TD>
</TR>
<TR align = "center">
    <TD> Singing </TD>
    <TD> Dancing </TD>
    <TD> Price Distribution </TD>
</TR>
</TABLE>
</BODY>
</HTML>
```

Or

(i) **autobuffer** This boolean attribute if specified, the video will automatically begin buffering even if it is not set to automatically play.

(ii) **width** This attribute specifies the width of the video display area in pixels.

(iii) **type** This attribute specifies the video file standard type.

6. MODEM stands for MOdulator/DEModulator. It is a hardware device that enables a computer to send and receive information over telephone lines by converting the digital data used by your computer into an analog signal used on telephone lines and then converting back once received on the other end.

Or

The backbone of the World Wide Web is made up of files or documents called web pages, that contains information and links to resources both text and multimedia.

The web page provides the information to the clients about his factory of spare parts. Moreover, he can receive the order on the Internet from the clients using the web page.

7. Search engine is a website that provides the required data on specific topics. It turns the web into a powerful tool for finding information on any topic.

For searching any particular information, following steps are to be taken

Step 1 Go to the home page of the search engine.

Step 2 On the home page, a text box will appear somewhere.

Step 3 In that textbox, type a keyword that you want to search.

Step 4 After that, there will be a button that looks like an image and has the word search written on it. Clicking on that button, search will start and will bring up a new web page with a list of websites related to that topic.

Step 5 Clicking on one of the links in the list will access that website.

Or

Differences between web browser and web server are as follows

Web browser	Web server
Web browser is a software which is used to browse and display pages available over Internet.	Web server is a software which provides these documents when requested by web browsers.
A web browser sends request to server for web based documents and services.	Web server sees and approves those requests made by web browsers and sends the document in response.
Web browser sends an HTTP Request and gets a HTTP Response.	Web server receives HTTP Request and sends a HTTP Response.
Web browser has no processing model.	Web server follows three major processing models: process based, thread based or hybrid.
Web browsers stores user data in cookies in local machine.	Web server provide an area to store the website.
e.g. Google Chrome.	e.g. Apache Server.

8. Following is the HTML code to generate the given web page

```
<HTML>
<HEAD><TITLE> Painting Exhibition in India
</TITLE></HEAD>
        <BODY alink="orange" vlink="red">
<FONT face="times new roman"  color="red">
<H1 align="left"> Painting Exhibition in India
</H1>
</FONT>
<IMG src="paint1.jpg" align="right"
width="150" height="150">
<FONT size="4" face="calibri">\
```

Painting is basically an art of applying paint, pigment, color or other elements with the help of brush, knives, sponges or airbrushes to any surface. Under our roof you will find large assortments of unmatched paintings with creative style statement. `<BR>`

Paintings can be done on the surfaces of walls, paper and many more to deliver creative art style of the painter. The broad spectra of paintings can be easily classified into contemporary paintings, nature paintings, modern paintings and many more according to the painter's art style.

```
</FONT>
<TABLE border="3" align="center"
bordercolor="blue">
<CAPTION color="red"> Available Paintings
</CAPTION>
        <TR>
<TD rowspan="5"> I <BR> N <BR> D <BR> I <BR>
A <BR> N </TD>
<TD colspan="3"> PAINTING </TD>
        </TR>
        <TR>
                <TH> NAME </TH>
                <TH> QTY </TH>
                <TH> PRIZE </TH>
        </TR>
        <TR>
            <TD> Oil Painting </TD>
            <TD> 4 </TD>
            <TD> 3000 </TD>
        </TR>
        <TR>
            <TD> Glass Painting </TD>
```

```
        <TD> 2 </TD>
        <TD> 5000 </TD>
     </TR>
     <TR>
        <TD> Canvas </TD>
        <TD> 2 </TD>
        <TD> 1000 </TD>
     </TR>
   </TABLE><BR>
```
<A href="inquiry@abc.com"> For more inquiry
Click here </A>
```
        </BODY>
</HTML>
```
Or

If you are on a web page and see the colored and/or an underlined text, it is a hyperlink. It is also known as hypertext link or just link. By default, color of a hyperlink is blue.

Hyperlinks are the links that carry user from one web page to another. It is activated by clicking on an underlined text or image. In HTML, links can be created by using <A> anchor tag. <A> tag is a container tag that means it requires a starting as well as ending tag.

There are two types of linking in a web page as follows

(i) **External linking** It refers to a different page on a different website. When a user clicks on a hyperlink on a web page, user is directed on the location, which is specified in that hyperlink. To create an external link with <A> tag and its href attribute, a title attribute also needed.

(ii) **Internal linking** This is a type of HTML linking that links pages within a single website, various sections of same document or different document. To create an internal link, you need to use a pair of <A> tags. The first <A> tag is used to specify the name of the target location for identification purpose. The second <A> tag is used to create a link to the target fragment.

Practice Paper 2*
(Solved)

General Instructions

■ **Time :** 2 Hours
■ **Max. Marks :** 25

1. There are 8 questions in the question paper. All questions are compulsory.
2. Question no. 1 is a Case Based Question, which has five MCQs. Each question carries one mark.
3. Question no. 2-6 are Short Answer Type Questions. Each question carries 2 marks.
4. Question no. 7-8 are Long Answer Type Questions. Each question carries 5 marks.
5. There is no overall choice. However, internal choices have been provided in some questions. Students have to attempt only one of the alternatives in such questions.

** As exact Blue-print and Pattern for CBSE Term II exams is not released yet. So the pattern of this paper is designed by the author on the basis of trend of past CBSE Papers. Students are advised not to consider the pattern of this paper as official, it is just for practice purpose.*

1. Direction *Read the following passage and answer the questions that follows.*

It refers to an electronic mode of delivering learning, training or educational programs to users.

E-learning is the mode of acquiring knowledge by means of Internet and computer based training programs. E-learning can be done anywhere and at anytime.

The modules of E-learning are designed to provide not only adequate and relevant information but also make learning highly engaging and interactive using multimedia.

Broadly, E-learning is synonymous with Computer Based Instruction, Computer Based Training, Internet Based Training, Web Based Training and online education. E-learning applications and processes include Web based learning, computer based learning, virtual classrooms and digital collaboration.

(i) The full form of CBI is
   (a) Computer Based Instruction
   (b) Computer Based Information
   (c) Computer Based Internet
   (d) Computer Based Infrastructure

(ii) Which of the following is/are categories of E-learning?
   (a) Synchronous
   (b) Asynchronous
   (c) Both (a) and (b)
   (d) None of these

(iii) E-learning includes
   (a) web based learning
   (b) computer based learning
   (c) virtual classroom
   (d) All of these

(iv) Synchronous means
   (a) at the same time
   (b) not at the same time
   (c) Both (a) and (b)
   (d) None of these

(v) .... helps us to learn anywhere using Internet.
  (a) E-learning
  (b) E-book
  (c) E-trading
  (d) None of these

2. Write the HTML code to send an E-mail to arihant@pub.com from your web page.

Or Write a code to link www. google.com page with text "Hello" and also show that title as "Click Here".

3. What do you mean by web client?

4. Observe the following table and write the HTML code to generate it.

Name	Subject
Riya	Science
Ansh	Mathematics
Rahul	Science
Aashi	English

5. What is chatting? Also, write about its basic modes.

Or Which protocol is used for creating a connection with a remote computer? Explain.

6. Write the full form of Cc and Bcc (used in E-mail communication). Explain the difference between them.

Or Briefly explain the significance of video conferencing.

7. Distinguish between WWW and Internet.

Or Discuss about mobile technologies with its related terms 3G and 4G.

8. Write the HTML code for the following output.

  (i) Title of the page should be Dubai Tourism.
 (ii) The heading text "WELCOME TO DUBAI" is in arial font and is of red color.
(iii) The horizontal lines below the heading are 6 pixels thick and of maroon color.
 (iv) Image used in the page is dubai.jpg.
  (v) The bulleted list contains links as specified below
      • The text Morning is of brown color.
      • The text Evening is of brown color.
 (vi) E-mail id for bottom message is dubai@gmail.com.

Or Write an HTML code to print the following table.

Student Details

Computer Application Class 10			
Student Name	**Roll No**	**Address**	**Percentage**
Amaya	1	Shastri Nagar	83
Aashi	2	T.P Nagar	78
Priyank	3	Saket	90
Vansh	4	Bypass	93

Note • Background color of a table is pink.
       • Caption of a table is in red color.

Explanations

1. (i) (*a*) The full form of CBI is Computer Based Instruction. CBI is any curricula in which students interact with a computer as a key element of the learning process.

(ii) (*c*) E-learning can be divided into two categories as follows

(a) **Synchronous** It means "at the same time".

(b) **Asynchronous** It means "not at the same time".

(iii) (*d*) E-learning is the mode of acquiring knowledge by means of Internet and computer based training programs. It includes web based learning, computer based learning and virtual classroom.

(iv) (*a*) Synchronous means "at the same time", interaction of participants with an instructor *via* the web in a real time.

(v) (*a*) E-learning refers to an electronic mode of delivering learning, training or educational programs to users. It helps us to learn anywhere using Internet.

2.
```
<HTML>
<BODY>
     <A href ="mailto : arihant@pub.com">
     arihant@pub.com</A>
</BODY>
</HTML>
```
Or
```
<HTML>
<BODY>
     <A href ="http://www.google.com"
      title = "Click Here">Hello</A>
```
```
</BODY>
</HTML>
```

3. Web client describes a special program designed as a user interface, through which messages are sent to a web server.

Web clients usually operate within a web browser window, although some are installed to a mobile or computer as downloadable software.

4.
```
<HTML>
<BODY>
<TABLE cellpadding = "10" cellspacing = "0"
border = "1">
<TR align = "center">
<TH> Name </TH>
<TH> Subject </TH>
</TR>
<TR align ="center">
<TD> Riya </TD>
<TD> Science </TD>
</TR>
<TR align = "center">
<TD> Ansh </TD>
<TD> Mathematics </TD>
</TR>
<TR align = "center">
<TD> Rahul </TD>
<TD> Science </TD>
</TR>
<TR align = "center">
```

```
<TD> Aashi </TD>
<TD> English </TD>
</TR>
</TABLE>
</BODY>
</HTML>
```

5. Chatting is a virtual means of communication that involves the sending and receiving of messages, share audios and videos between users located in any part of the world.

There are two basic modes for chatting on the Internet as follows

  (i) **Text based chat** enables communication through sending and receiving text messages.

  (ii) **Multimedia chat** enables communication through audio and video transmission.

Or

Telnet is a protocol used for creating a connection with a remote computer. Once your telnet client establishes a connection to the remote host, telnet client becomes a virtual terminal, allowing you to communicate with the remote host from your computer. It provides an error free connection, which is always faster than the latest conventional modems.

6. Cc stands for Carbon copy and Bcc stands for Blind carbon copy.

In Cc, all recipients will be able to see each other mail address. Whereas, in Bcc none of the recipient will be able to see each other mail address.

Or

  (i) Video conferencing reduces your travel costs by working remotely and also increases productivity through collaborative working.

  (ii) Many people can share their videos with each other at the same time.

7. Differences between WWW and Internet are as follows

WWW (World Wide Web)	Internet
The World Wide Web is the common system for navigating the Internet. It is not the only system that can be used for such access, but it is by far the most common one.	The Internet is a public network of network with amaze of wired and wireless connections between separate groups of servers computers and countless devices from around the world.
The World Wide Web is distinguished from other systems through its use of HTTP. It can be safely said that the HTTP is the language of the World Wide Web.	Along with Internets, there also exist the Intranets, which is the same type of information network but more privatized in order to control access.

WWW (World Wide Web)	Internet
The HTTP along with being the language of the World Wide Web also governs it by dealing with linking of files, documents and other resources.	The Internet is governed by a set of rules and regulations collectively known as Internet Protocol (IP). The IP deals with data transmitted through the Internet.
The invention of the World Wide Web can be credited to Sir Tim Berners Lee. During his work at the European Organization for Nuclear Research in 1989, he had developed the basic idea of the WWW to merge the evolving technologies of computers, data networks and hypertext into a powerful and easy to use global information system.	The first workable prototype of the Internet was the ARPANET (Advanced Research Project Agency Network) in the late 1960s. After its adoption on January 1st 1983, researchers began to develop a "network of networks" which evolved into the modern form of the Internet.
WWW is more software-oriented as compared to the Internet.	Internet is primarily hardware-based.

Or

Mobile technologies is a form of technology that is mostly used in cellular communication and other related aspects. It has improved from a simple device used for phone call and messaging into a multitasking device used for GPS navigation, instant messaging tool etc.

3G (Third Generation) 3G is short for Third Generation of mobile telecommunications technology also called Tri-Band 3G.

3G telecommunication networks support services that provide the information transfer rate of atleast 200 Kbps.

It adds multimedia facilities that allow video, audio and graphics applications. However, many services advertised as 3G provides higher speed than the minimum technical requirements for a 3G service.

4G (Fourth Generation) In telecommunications, 4G is the Fourth Generation of mobile phone communication standards. It is a successor of the Third Generation (3G) standard.

A 4G system provides mobile ultra-broadband Internet access. It is based on packet switching only and these systems are projected to provide speeds up to 100 Mbps while moving and 1 Gbps while stationary.

8.
```
<HTML>
<HEAD>
<TITLE> Dubai Tourism</TITLE>
</HEAD>
<BODY>
<CENTER>
<H1>
```

```
<FONT face = "arial"color = "red">
WELCOME TO DUBAI</FONT>
</H1>
</CENTER>
<HR width ="80%" size ="6"color ="maroon"
noshade>
<HR width = "60% "size = "6" color =
"maroon" noshade>
<P>
<FONT size = "5">
Enjoy the world of pure travel masti
</FONT>
<CENTER>
<IMG src = "dubai. jpg" height = "300"
width ="750">
</CENTER>
</P>
The following is a list of major tourist attraction in Dubai :
<BR><BR>
<UL type = "disc">
<LI><FONT color="brown">
Morning</FONT>
-Dolphinarium and Palm Dubai
</LI>
<LI><FONT color="brown">
Evening</FONT>
-Ski Dubai and Cruise
</LI>
</UL>
<CENTER> For enquires write at<FONT color =
"blue"> <U>
dubai@gmail.com</U></FONT></CENTER>
</BODY>
</HTML>
```

Or

```
<HTML>
<HEAD><TITLE>Student</TITLE></HEAD>
<BODY>
<table border="1" bgcolor="pink"
align="center">
<CAPTION> <B> <FONT size="4" color="red">
Student Details</FONT></B></CAPTION>
<TR>
<TH colspan="4" align="center">
Computer Application Class 10
<TH>
</TR>
<TR>
<TH>Student  Name</TH>
<TH>Roll No</TH>
<TH>Address</TH>
<TH>Percentage</TH>
</TR>
<TR>
<TD>Amaya</TD>
<TD>1</TD>
<TD>Shastri Nagar</TD>
<TD>83</TD>
</TR>
<TR>
<TD>Aashi</TD>
<TD>2</TD>
<TD>T.P Nagar</TD>
<TD>78</TD>
</TR>
<TR>
<td>Priyank</TD>
<td>3</TD>
<td>Saket</TD>
<td>90</TD>
</TR>
<TR>
<TD>Vansh</TD>
<TD>4</td>
<TD>Bypass</TD>
<TD>93</TD>
</TR>
</TABLE></BODY></HTML>
```

Practice Paper 3*
(Solved)

<table>
<tr><td>

General Instructions

1. There are 8 questions in the question paper. All questions are compulsory.
2. Question no. 1 is a Case Based Question, which has five MCQs. Each question carries one mark.
3. Question no. 2-6 are Short Answer Type Questions. Each question carries 2 marks.
4. Question no. 7-8 are Long Answer Type Questions. Each question carries 5 marks.
5. There is no overall choice. However, internal choices have been provided in some questions. Students have to attempt only one of the alternatives in such questions.

</td><td>

■ **Time :** 2 Hours
■ **Max. Marks :** 25

</td></tr>
</table>

** As exact Blue-print and Pattern for CBSE Term II exams is not released yet. So the pattern of this paper is designed by the author on the basis of trend of past CBSE Papers. Students are advised not to consider the pattern of this paper as official, it is just for practice purpose.*

1. **Direction** *Read the following passage and answer the questions that follows*

Chat is the online textual or multimedia conversation. It is a real-time communication between two users *via* computer. It is widely interactive text-based communication process that takes place over the Internet.

Chatting is a virtual means of communication that involves the sending and receiving of messages, share audios and videos between users located in any part of the world.

In chatting, you type a message in your chat box, which is immediately received by the recipient, then the recipient types a message in response to your message, which is instantly received by you.

(i) Which of the following is/are popular chat application(s)?
    (a) WhatsApp   (b) WeChat
    (c) Tango   (d) All of these

(ii) It enables communication through sending and receiving text messages.
    (a) Text based chat   (b) Multimedia chat
    (c) Both (a) and (b)   (d) None of these

(iii) A/An .... is the hub of Internet chatting.
    (a) chat space   (b) chat place
    (c) chat room   (d) chat group

(iv) Chat is the online .... conversation.
    (a) textual   (b) multimedia
    (c) Both (a) and (b)   (d) None of these

(v) You can share .... using chat.
    (a) messages   (b) audio
    (c) video   (d) All of these

2. Write a code to display the text "Contact Us" should be linked with arihant@pub.com E-mail id.

3. What do you mean by web address?

Or Write any two advantages and disadvantages of chat.

4. Write output of the following HTML code.

```
<HTML>
<HEAD> <TITLE> Table </TITLE></HEAD>
<BODY>
<TABLE border = "1" cellpadding = "1" cellspacing = "4">
<TR>
<TD align = "center" colspan = "3" > Cell A </TD>
</TR>
<TR>
<TD> rowspan = "2" > Cell B </TD>
<TD> Cell C </TD>
<TD> Cell D</TD>
</TR>
<TR>
<TD> Cell E </TD>
<TD> Cell F </TD>
</TR>
</TABLE>
</BODY>
</HTML>
```

Or Write the code to embed audio in a web page.

5. What steps should be followed to setup an Internet connection?

6. What are the roles of rowspan and colspan attributes? Explain with suitable HTML example.

Or How is external linking different from internal linking?

7. Distinguish between web page and website.

Or What is E-banking? Also, write two categories of E-banking.

8. Observe the following table and write the HTML code to generate it.

Activities	
Group A	Dancing
	Singing
	Yoga
Group B	Gymnastic
	Acting
	Fashion Show
Group C	Quiz
	Robotics
	Crafting

Or Write the code to generate the following web page.

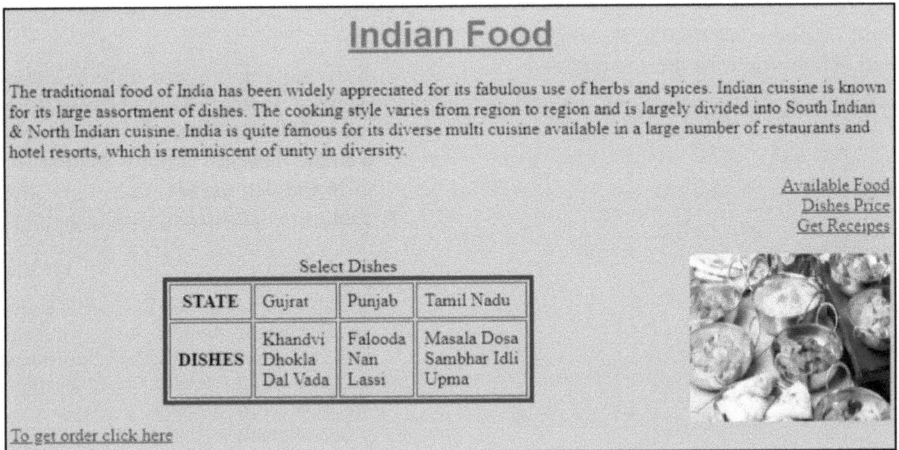

STATE	Gujrat	Punjab	Tamil Nadu
DISHES	Khandvi Dhokla Dal Vada	Falooda Nan Lassi	Masala Dosa Sambhar Idli Upma

The following points while generating the web page

(i) Title of the page is "Indian Food".

(ii) Link color is blue, vlink color is brown and alink color is pink.

(iii) Font face of heading is "arial".

(iv) The color of the heading of the page is green.

(v) Image used as indian.jpg.

(vi) Table border is 4px and border color is maroon.

(vii) Use link as:

For Available Food as food1.html

For Dishes Price as food2. html

For Get Recipes as food3. html

(viii) E-mail id for bottom message "To get order click here" as inquiry@abc.com.

Explanations

1. (i) (*d*) WhatsApp, WeChat, Tango are popular chat applications. These applications involve the sending and receiving of messages, share audios and videos between users located in any part of the world.

(ii) (*a*) Text based chat enables communication through sending and receiving text messages.

(iii) (*c*) A chat room is the hub of Internet chatting. Chat rooms are actually Chat servers that allow several users to login to them simultaneously.

(iv) (*c*) Chat is the online textual or multimedia conversation. It is a real time communication between two users *via* computer.

(v) (*d*) You can share messages, audio and video using chat, between users located in any part of the world.

2.
```
<HTML>
<BODY>
        <A href = "mailto :
```
```
arihant@pub.com">Contact Us </A>

</BODY>
</HTML>
```

3. Web is a collection of documents (web pages) stored on computers around the world. Each web page has an address describing where it can be found. This address is known as web address or URL (Uniform Resource Locator). Every computer connected to the Internet has its unique web address, without which it cannot be reached by other computers.

Or

Advantages of Chat

(i) Photos can be sent using an instant messaging.

(ii) Emotions can be expressed easily when communicating with a person.

Disadvantages of Chat

   (i) Viruses can be easily spread *via* texting.
  (ii) Children tend to spend more time in chatting with
       friends instead of bonding with their family and
       studies.

4.

Cell A		
Cell B	Cell C	Cell D
	Cell E	Cell F

Or

```
<HTML>
<BODY>
<AUDIO controls autoplay>
<SOURCE src = "/ html/audio.ogg"
type = "audio/ogg"/>
<SOURCE src = "/html/audio.wav"
         type = "audio/wav"/>
Your browser does not support the <AUDIO>
element.
</AUDIO>
</BODY>
</HTML>
```

5. To setup an Internet connection, do the following steps

Step 1 Connect the necessary hardware like modem,
         ethernet cable etc., and run necessary softwares
         such as LAN driver.

Step 2 Make a preliminary connection using ethernet cable
         or a wireless connection.

Step 3 Go to the router's default IP address.

Step 4 Setup the Internet connection using login name and
         password, which is provided by the ISP.

Step 5 Save your settings.

6. colspan attribute allows the user to stretch a cell to span
    multiple columns (merge two or more columns). rowspan
    attribute is used to span multiple rows (merge two or
    more rows).

   e.g.
```
<TABLE border = '1'>
<TR>
<TD> Row-1 Column-1 </TD>
<TD colspan = "2"> Row-1 Column-2 and 3
                             </TD>
<TD rowspan = "2"> Row-1 and 2 Column-4
                          </TD> </TR>
<TR>
<TD> Row-2 Column-1 </TD>
<TD> Row-2 Column-2 </TD>
<TD> Row-2 Column-3 </TD>
```

```
</TR>
</TABLE>
```

Or

External link is a type of linking that goes to another
website. It is a linking of two different documents. While,
internal linking is a type of linking that links pages within
a single website, various sections of same document or
different documents.

7. Differences between web page and website are as follows

Web page	Website
A web page is defined as the smaller part of the website that includes contents like text, media, etc. It also comprises links to many other relevant web pages.	A website is a cluster of different web pages of different topics addressed to certain URLs.
It is a single document that is displayed by the web browser using a specific URL address.	It is a collection of many documents. Web browsers are used to access such documents using specific URL addresses attached to the website.
Web page usually contains content regarding a single entity type.	A website usually contains content regarding several entities.
It is an individual hypertext document linked under a website.	It is a collection of multiple pages hosted on the server.
It is used to store the contents or resources that are to be displayed on a website.	It is a place that is used to display the content.
It is comparatively less-complex to develop because it is just a smaller part of the website.	It is comparatively more complex to develop.
It requires less time for development as it is not complex, like a website.	It requires comparatively more time for development.

Or

E-banking is defined as the automated delivery of new
and traditional banking products and services directly to
the customers through an electronic and interactive
communication channels. E-banking is also known as
Internet banking.

E-banking can be broadly classified into two categories,
which are as follows

   (i) **Transactional** It involves performing financial
       transactions. Transactional activities are as follows

       ▪ Electronic fund transfer

       ▪ Bill payments

       ▪ Loan applications and repayments

- Buying investment products

(ii) **Non-transactional** It involves viewing bank statements. Non-transactional activities are as follows

- Account balance viewing
- Bank statement downloading
- Cheque book ordering
- Provision of account/bank statement

8.
```
<HTML>
<BODY>
<TABLE border = "1" bordercolor ="black"
cellspacing = "0">
<CAPTION> Activities </CAPTION>
<TR>
<TD rowspan ="3"> Group A </TD>
<TD> Dancing </TD>
</TR>
<TR>
<TD> Singing </TD>
</TR>
<TR>
<TD> Yoga </TD>
</TR>
<TR>
<TD rowspan = "3"> Group B </TD>
<TD> Gymnastic </TD>
</TR>
<TR>
<TD> Acting </TD>
</TR>
<TR>
<TD> Fashion Show </TD>
</TR>
<TR>
<TD rowspan = "3"> Group C </TD>
<TD> Quiz </TD>
</TR>
<TR>
<TD> Robotics </TD>
</TR>
<TR>
<TD> Crafting </TD>
</TR>
</TABLE>
</BODY>
```

```
</HTML>
```

Or

```
<HTML>
<HEAD><TITLE> Indian Food </TITLE></HEAD>
<BODY link="blue" vlink="brown"
alink="pink" bgcolor="orange">
<FONT face="arial" color="green">
<H1 align="center"><U> Indian Food </U></H1>
</FONT>
```

The traditional food of India has been widely appreciated for its fabulous use of herbs and spices. Indian cuisine is known for its large assortment of dishes.

The cooking style varies from region to region and is largely divided into South Indian & North Indian cuisine. India is quite famous for its diverse multi cuisine available in a large number of restaurants and hotel resorts, which is reminiscent of unity in diversity.

```
<P align="right"><A href="food1. html">
```
Available Food </A>

```
<A href="food2.html"> Dishes Price </A><BR>
<A href="food3.html"> Get Receipes </A></P>
<IMG src="indian.jpg" align="right" width
="180" height="150">
<TABLE border="4" bordercolor="maroon"
cellpadding="6" align="center">
<CAPTION> Select Dishes </CAPTION>
<TR>
        <TH> STATE </TH>
        <TD> Gujrat </TD>
        <TD> Punjab </TD>
        <TD> Tamil Nadu </TD>
</TR>
 <TR>
        <TH> DISHES </TH>
        <TD> Khandvi <BR> Dhokla <BR> Dal
                        Vada<\TD>
        <TD> Falooda <BR> Nan <BR> Lassi </TD>
        <TD> Masala Dosa <BR> Sambhar Idli
                        <BR> Upma </TD>
</TR>
</TABLE>
<BR>
<A href="inquiry@abc.com"> To get order click
here </A>
</BODY>
</HTML>
```

Printed by Libri Plureos GmbH in Hamburg,
Germany